FREEDOM
IS A GIFT
OF GOD

Freedomisagiftofgod.com
Freedomforall99@hotmail.com

FREEDOM IS A GIFT OF GOD

✦

*America and the
American immigrants*

Yonas R. Berhane

iUniverse, Inc.
Bloomington

FREEDOM IS A GIFT OF GOD
America and the American immigrants

iUniverse books may be ordered through booksellers or by contacting:

iUniverse
1663 Liberty Drive
Bloomington, IN 47403
www.iuniverse.com
1-800-Authors (1-800-288-4677)

ISBN: 978-0-595-48392-1 (sc)
ISBN: 978-0-595-60483-8 (e)
ISBN: 978-0-595-71817-7 (hc)

Printed in the United States of America

iUniverse rev. date: 08/31/2012

Contents

Acknowledgment

I dedicate this book to my grandmother
HAREGU W/MICHAEL
For raising me throughout a tough time and believing in me
for who I am.

I'd also like to thank God, and I am also enormously grateful
for the love and hope from my beautiful kids
ESKENDER YONAS and DELENA YONAS

I have left out so many family members and friends. I hope
they know how much I love them and appreciate their support.
As always, thank you to Edna Cardenas for helping me
to make this book possible

Ms. Barbara Washburn: thank you for your help.
I really appreciate you for volunteering your time for me
and for others whom English is their second language.

And thank you toMike Valentino for editing my grammar
and spelling; learn from me and allowing me to learn from him.

Introduction

As an immigrant to America, I had some difficulty making decisions. Each one made an impact on my life which I was forced to accept or embrace. Things were very different than when I was living at home. When you live with your immediate family, it can be assumed that life is easy. You have the blessing of a built-in support group. You can seek help with tough decisions. But as an immigrant, you usually wind up pretty much on your own. The comfort of having family with me was gone the moment I departed on the airplane. But one thing I do know is that God is always with me. Wherever I go and whatever I do, I know that he is looking out for me. I believe that strong faith drives the purpose of my life.

Taking control of your life, of course, is not always easy, but you have to face the challenge sooner or later. You have to learn how you can overcome all of the challenges that you will inevitably face. Everything happens for a reason, and for me the chance that I was granted in coming to America was an opportunity which many people throughout the world would love to have.

When I arrived in America my life changed dramatically. My first year was so exciting. I appreciated freedom and the friendship that I received from society. It made my life joyous, despite the fact that I landed in America with one piece of luggage and some change in my pocket--maybe just enough for a rainy day. Beyond that I didn't had anything. I don't know where to start and where to finish; it was a long journey. There were many obstacles I had to overcome, such as adapting to the American way of life. Nonetheless, I accomplished much, including such blessings as becoming the father of two wonderful and beautiful kids. I have also always been a firm believer in God, which helped me reconnect with my older brother and friends here in the United States.

My older brother left home when I was a little boy. He left home for the same reason I chose to leave my family behind: the dangerous political and social environment where we were living. By the time I arrived in America, I hadn't seen my brother in almost fifteen years. We were not close brothers. Sometimes he seemed mean and bossy, but my grandmother always helped me to understand that my brother was looking out for me. I had that strong desire to feel like we belong to something greater, I guess we were blessed by our grandmother. We were lucky enough to be raised by our wonderful grandmother, whom we loved very much. She was a humble, caring, and special person.

I learned how to conquer my past, my pain, and the things that were keeping me from moving forward. I say rest in peace to my grandmother. She was my father and my mother, an incredible and amazing person, and everything to me. When I lost her, I was devastated. I felt like I had holes in my shoes. It was extremely uncomfortable dealing with the loss of my grandmother. Nothing felt the same. I was helplessly lost, but I learned that I had to leave it behind. I had to move on.

For me, writing a book was a difficult task, but I was convinced that I could do it and even with my limited ability, I did indeed write it. Even though English is my second language, I didn't let that stop me. I forced myself to learn and to associate with all kinds of people. I read books and newspapers. I believe you do not really understand something unless you are forced to communicate it in a simple way. I wrote this book to share with the American people my experience, my perspective, and my passion for freedom.

In life we have to break free from destructive emotions, anger, and resentment. These days we allow fear to take over our lives because of terror threats and the anxiety of an uncertain economy, among other things. I fully recognize that the world seems to be heading toward more hate, greed, and complex problems. On the other hand, our enemies intend to disrupt our freedom and people kill each other for their insane ideologies. Those who offer hate and destruction like terrorists and dictators are evil.

An evil leader's agenda usually involves the destruction of human rights and, in many cases, the decimation of certain "problematic" groups. All of this in favor of their own power and beliefs.

We may not be able to stop or defeat all evil, but if we come together and respect one another, no matter what our religion or ethnicity, and treat everyone the same way that we want to be treated. These are but a few of the qualities that we need in order to demonize evil. Man has always been seeking his liberty and rights since the earliest days of civilization. America, throughout its history, has had a commitment to freedom through good times and bad times, through peace, and through war.

We adore freedom because it's our God-given right. Freedom guarantees the inalienable rights of life, liberty, and the pursuit of happiness. When we think about freedom, we should not always think only about ourselves. We should also demand freedom for people who need it most. There are great numbers of people who are demanding freedom both inside and outside of the United States, including immigrants who live in the United States, whether documented or undocumented. Some are living under the shadow of tyranny. What should we do about their freedom?

In the pages that follow, I explain what it's like to be an immigrant. Immigrants came here for the same reason I came here: for the opportunities available in a free capitalistic society and to cherish freedom.

America can be a lawful society as well as a welcoming country. We must uphold the American tradition, faith, and values. In seeking to follow God, we must first come to terms with our human condition. The idea of welcoming strangers is a very basic form of Christianity. I know some people will proclaim that they are Christian, but where is our belief and what is the purpose of our Christianity if it is not to pursue God's message? Most immigrants seek freedom and an escape from dictators and religious intolerance in order to find a better place to work and to raise their families. We have to open our arms to those who need our help; we need to be understanding, compassionate, and generous.

This book is far more than just my personal story. My views are focused on a positive perspective of America and how America is a great country for all of us. I would like my book to serve as an *eye opener* to some extent, revealing stories that the American public is unaware of. It will help us to come together, to respect one another, and to learn how to respect one another's cultures and values.

Instead of being on a constant terrorist watch, we could regain free movement within our society. Terror threats will be a thing of the past.

Coming to America

On March 26, 1994, I woke up a little earlier than usual. It was a wonderful day. The sun was bright, and I went outside to enjoy its lovely rays. I was walking on the side of the road, and I could hear the birds chirping. They were flying from one tree to another tree, as if they were playing in the light.

While I was enjoying my day, I ran into one of my friends. He saw me from across the street and came over and asked me how I was doing. We exchanged a few words on our way to a little breakfast place, where we sat down for doughnuts and cappuccino.

We were reminiscing about good times, and, all of a sudden, he remembered that I had been given a chance recently to go to America and asked me when I was going.

"I'm leaving tomorrow" I said.

He was shocked… "Are you really leaving tomorrow?"

He kept asking me over and over, and I smiled.

Yes, I said, "tomorrow, I will be on way to America."

If I do not see you again then "I wish you good luck, my friend," he said with a big smile on his face.

He added, "Hey, when you get to America, please do not forget about me."

I assured him that I would never forget about him.

"Matter of fact," I said, "the day I get to America, I will write you a letter" thank you, he replied gratefully.

For some reason it seemed that he did not hear what I was saying, and his face expression changed. His voice got lower at the same time he got choked up.

I could barely hear him as he said, "Please don't forget about me."

I assured him again that I'm going to keep my promise.

My friend's big smile disappeared in an instant, and I could see tear-drops falling from his eyes.

"What's wrong?" I asked him.

"You know what is wrong," he said. "I will be left behind."

I knew exactly what he meant.

Why not me!

Indeed, that was the reason for his tears. Wiping his eyes, he said, "God please give me a chance to cherish freedom."

I told him that his dream to see freedom for you and the people he loved would someday come true.

I told him again that the future need not seem so bleak......

"There are better days ahead, my friend," I said.

Well, he broke my heart when I saw him crying, pleading for his freedom.

I understand why he felt that way; we were all living under the same circumstance of life with no hope, no choice, and no freedom. That is the hardest, cruelest way for any human being to have to live.

I shook his hand and embraced him and told him I was going to keep in touch with him and not to worry, that everything was going to be all right. He thanked me for giving him hope. I told him that my family was having a farewell party for me, and I invited him.

That night everybody got together for my farewell party: my family, friends, and all the other people I knew.

Everyone was dancing, laughing, just having a great time and remembering all of the good times that we had spent together. Towards the end of the party, everyone came to me and wished me good luck. They were hugging me and crying, and I responded in the same way.

There were mixed feelings--all the dancing and laughing turned into sadness. It was heartbreaking, but I had to deal with it because I chose to leave my family behind. I was leaving my homeland for the simple reason that I wanted to live in a land of freedom and opportunity. They made me feel that I was leaving them forever. But the chance to come to America was the opportunity that everybody wanted. I could not let this opportunity slip through my hands.

I come from a society of hard-working people. Let me tell you this: we lived under a dictatorship where we did not have any choice but to follow their rules and laws. The dictators gave us one choice, and that choice was whatever they said, we had to accept. Do not ask, and do not tell. If we asked anything more than we should, we might face serious consequences such as jail time or torture.

After the farewell party, thinking about the good times we had, I went to my room to get some sleep. I woke before 6:00 am, the sheets all tangled around my legs. I had a lot on my mind. I couldn't get back to sleep. Before I went to bed, I packed my belongings, and, in my wallet, I had a picture of Jesus Christ. I reached out for a candle, and I laid the picture next to the candle. I lit the candle and knelt down to pray. I said to my Lord, "Thanks, God, for giving me this chance. Thanks, God, for showing me a way out of this horrible life. Thanks, God, for giving me this opportunity and for blessing me.

I woke up the next morning, and I took a shower to refresh myself. My family members and friends were waiting on me to go to the airport. When we got to the airport, we exchanged a few words, and we said goodbye to each other.

As soon as I got to the terminal, an old, tall man with dark skin and a long beard approached me and asked me my name.

"Yonas," I said. He introduced himself and asked me where I was going.

"America," I replied.

He smiled at me. "You are a lucky young man," he said.

"Yes, I'm lucky. Thanks to God, I have this chance to be in America." I said.

I lived in America for six years, he said. "It is a great country." As he was walking by my side, he ran his fingers through his beard and said, "America is a good place to make a living and go to school. It's also a land of full of opportunity, a land where you can live by your own free choices".

"You can speak your mind without fear. As soon as you arrive in America, you will see the difference between living with and without freedom. I want you to do one thing. Go to school and work hard, do not fool yourself with materialistic things."

I told him that I would try to do my best, and he asked me one more thing. "What do you want to do when you get to America?"

"First of all, I just want to see what America looks like, and I want to work and make a good living," I said.

"That is not what I expect to hear from you," he said while he was walking. He grew silent for a moment and then he turned around and said, "Like I told you, I want you to go to school, work hard, and use this opportunity that you cannot get here."

At first I was thinking of going to America to see big cities and big buildings and crowds of people just like I used to see in the movies. I was anxious to meet wrestling and movie stars; this was a big deal for me at my young age.

But after I saw how serious his expression was, I realized that I had to pay attention. In that moment, I felt like I had been hit by a hammer.

To me it was basically a wakeup call. "Well," I said, "I may not be saying it the right way but my wish is to go to school. After I have educated myself, I want to help my family. I will try to do everything I can to help to sustain them. I also want to use my skills to help my people."

He said, "That is what I'm talking about," and smiled.

That smile told me a lot.

He wished me good luck on my flight. "Thank you," I said, and I knew I would never forget him.

As I walked on ahead, I kept looking back towards him because I felt like he was an angel. All the sadness that I had welled up inside of me because I was leaving my family and friends washed away in that moment with him.

I departed Bole international Airport. The flight was the longest flight of my entire life. We flew from Addis to London. Heathrow international Airport, this was the biggest Airport that I had ever seen.

I did not know anybody when I got there, and I felt lost for a moment. I tried to read every sign I saw so I could see where I was going.

The Flight attendants announced that we were going to spend the night in London and fly out the next morning. I was happy because that gave me a chance to see London overnight.

A shuttle bus took us to the hotel, and, as soon as we arrived, they gave us keys to our rooms. I know in my country they would have given me a regular key, unlike this one, which was a plastic card. So I wondered and asked how I would open the door with that. I had never seen a plastic card key like that before. Then, they smiled and came up and helped me open my room.

The first thing I did was turn on the T.V, playing with the remote. I flipped through channels over and over again and kept seeing different television programs. I was so excited because I had never had the chance to see so many channels. Where I came from during Mengustu Hailemariam regime, we only had one channel with a news program and a little bit of entertainment. The government manipulates and controls the media and uses it for propaganda.

When our plane arrived at the Dulles International Airport in Washington, D.C., I was welcomed by my older brother and one of my brother's close friends. We started driving towards his place, and he asked me how my flight was. I told him it was beautiful and told him what had happened in London. I also told him how I was having a good time and was very excited.

"How is the family back home?" he asked.

"Everyone is fine," I said.

The whole time we were in the car, I kept asking myself if we were really here in America, since what I saw in movies about America looked really different.

I thought I would be seeing tall buildings and crowds of people. Instead, I just saw one single, long road which I soon found out was what they call a highway.

My brother woke up the next day, and he went to work, and I did not have a chance to spend time with him. I realized how life was busy. He asked me later if I wanted to start working or go to school. I told him I wanted to work and make some money, so then I could go to school. He agreed and found me a job after a few days. I found the American system was wide open, and I became part of it.

My first year in America was so exciting. I met different people, and everyone was friendly and greeted me. I was enjoying myself. I thought to myself, "America really is a free country." I was not questioned by any law enforcement or any kind of officials, and to me, it was just me and my own world.

One of my first impressions of America was when I took the subway. Everybody was waiting to catch a train. A young lady approached me and asked,

"Is the Metro going to Virginia or D.C?"

"I don't know," I said. "I do not speak English."

She looked serious and said, "How long have you been In America?" I said "About two months." Then she said, "Welcome to America."

And I say "Thank you."

"Listen, do not be ashamed yourself. Try to force yourself and make an effort to speak." She could tell I could speak a little English and told me that language is a way to communicate each other.

She told me not to say that I did not speak any English, and then she said, "You see, now, you have spoken to me in a little English." and I realized that she was right. "If you keep making the effort," she said, "I'm sure that you will learn."

At first I was not sure why she approached me. I have to be honest, I was nervous, but I soon came to realize that she just wanted to help me. I thanked her for encouraging me. I was in awe. This person had just met me and did not know me, but spent time with me, and that made the biggest impression.

At that time I felt empowered; I lifted my head and knew that I was part of the society. It's hard to describe what kind of feeling I had at that time. I was so happy that I had been given a chance to feel right with society. I began to learn about the American culture and how they are very welcoming people who are humble and polite. They approached me with respect wherever I went.

In fact, I found it to be an enjoyable experience. They made me feel great and exceptional. I do not have enough words to talk about how great the American people are. I'm convinced this country is home for me, and I'm very comfortable here. I remember this famous quote "where you from is where you at." I have come to understand it is true: where you live is home.

I embrace that. I'm here now, and I feel blessed to be here in the land of opportunity.

I have been able to find myself in America. I have come to understand that, if I follow my instinct, I can reach my goals and my dreams. I have what is best for me and my family. I did not have this chance where I came from.

Freedom is the ultimate choice for human beings because it allows us the ability to choose how we want to live our lives. People, who are born with freedom, do not always appreciate the liberties that they have. How can they? They haven't experienced the lack of them. But people who are born without freedom always fight to hold onto whatever freedom they have. They have tasted the bitterness of a repressed life, and so they cherish the sweetness of the free one.

I was driving a limo for a living in Washington, D.C., which afforded me the opportunity to talk with a lot of people. I remember when I got a call to pick up my clients, and they were friendly and fun. I found them to be a great couple, and they seemed so happy. We got into the subject of why I was in America, as they were wondering why I left the country of my birth. I had to admit that was a good question.

"I just wanted to live in a free society," I said. The man asked me, "So how are things going for you in this country?"

"Things are going very well, thank you," I told him, and he was glad to hear that.

It was a beautiful day. As we waited at a red light, I could see the Thomas Jefferson Memorial and the Lincoln Memorial nearby.

"I think Washington is loaded with politicians," I said.

"You are absolutely right," she said with little smile on her face.

"Ma'am, do you like politics?" I asked to his wife. "Not so much," she replied, looking at her man with a grin, "unlike my husband."

So her husband squeezed into the middle and said, "Listen, Yonas. Politics affect you and your life in a direct or indirect way, so you have to be aware of it. That's why I am."

I said, "Well, it is a great lesson, but if you were in my shoes you would understand what politics means to me."

He shook his head. "I'm not sure what you mean by that," he said.

I told him that I do not speak good English, and I don't know why that came up first on my head.

"You speak good English, and I like your accent," he replied. But then he added, "I can understand that you want to tell me something, so I want to know all."

I told him, "As you know, I come from a different part of the world. We do not discuss politics much and we do not have freedom of speech, and we do not have the right to ask how or why. If we ask, we get in trouble, so, for me, it is a difficult thing to talk about politics."

His wife then said, "That's interesting." Then, after thinking about it for a moment, she asked, "So are you happy to be here?"

"Yes, ma'am I'm happy here," I explained. "And I'm glad to have the choices that I have here."

"I'm happy," she said. "You are a good man, and I hope that everything works out for you."

I smiled. "Everything will work out for me," I said. "I hope that the people that I have left behind will get the same chance I have."

Her husband then said, "It must be very bad over there. I replied, "Yes, sir."

"The bad thing is staying far away from home" I continued. "But that's the price you pay for freedom"

Then I turned around, and I said, "Can I ask you a question?"

"Go ahead" he said.

"Have you been anywhere in Africa or Asia?"

"Not really, but I have been to Tunisia once." he replied. "I'll tell you one thing I noticed; life in Tunisia was not easy for a lot of people," he said.

"Well, you are very lucky, sir, to have been born in America. Here the government stands and works for its own people. We do not have that where I come from, but I'm lucky enough to have it here." I said.

They were good people, and they listened to me intently. They soon understood where I came from so well that they came to a profound appreciation of the differences between being born here and being born outside of the United States. I believe that they truly appreciated what I had said to them. The couple embraced me warmly and said, "We are glad to have you here."

When we got to the restaurant, they invited me to have dinner with them, as always. I told them "Thank you, but I am working. Enjoy your dinner. I will be waiting outside for you."

They had a great sense of humor, and they were very generous and good people. God bless them wherever they are. I hope that I am able to meet up with them again one day.

I do not think that any American can appreciate being an American until they see what another world looks like. Other world leaders abuse their own people, torture them, and take their rights and freedom away. It is hard to imagine how they survive. I know a little bit about the efforts of European and American countries to help these people and how a lot of them seem to be better off than they used to be, but there is a lot more work to do.

According to the United States Department of State, East Africa's human rights record is poor. The governments restrict freedom of speech and press, the right to privacy, freedom of assembly, freedom of religion, freedom of movement, and workers' rights. Security forces commit serious human rights abuses, including arbitrary arrests and detentions, disappearances, and torture. The judicial system is weak; human rights groups are not allowed to conduct investigations; female genital mutilation is a widespread practice; child labor is common; and women, as well as ethnic minorities, are widely discriminated against.

This is why I left home: to search for freedom. I thank God for the opportunity. Now I have two beautiful children, and I have worked my way through from busboy to being an author. What more can I ask for.

God bless America.

America and the American Immigrants

It is well known that there are millions of immigrants in America. In fact, America has taken in more immigrants than any other nation on earth and has more immigrants than any other country in recorded history. These days, over 11 million immigrants in the United States have entered and continue to live here as undocumented immigrants, so-called illegal immigrants.

I am one of the millions of documented immigrants in this country; however, I disagree with those who call undocumented immigrants "illegal." I consider it a misnomer. There is nobody in this world born to be illegal. Everybody in God's eyes is legal. The only thing that makes the current immigrants "illegals" is that the laws of our time became far more harsh and difficult than they were in previous generations. People flow to America from different countries for one simple reason, to cherish freedom, to improve their lives, and to partake of the opportunities available in a free, capitalistic society.

When I entered America as an immigrant, the law required me to apply for the permanent resident permit, known as the green card. The process involved in approving or disapproving of green cards is pretty much a matter of luck. The system is insufficient because it does not read an immigrant's heart and soul. There is no subjective standard. The immigration system in place does not recognize the immigrant's motives. It is assumed the motive is strictly economic, but that isn't always necessarily true. I know a lot of immigrants because of insufficient immigration law caught in the middle with a little option to follow up the process. Some of them get deported, and a lot of them are living without papers, making them part of the growing horde of "illegals."

Most immigrants come here to fulfill their dreams. They also have an array of opportunities and freedoms they did not have in their home countries. With this immigration application form, it seems that this dream could slip from their hands. Most would not agree to leave America, but would try to stay in hopes of getting another chance. For me, this is where the government and the immigrants do not see eye-to eye.

The government may not give them another chance but the immigrants keep hoping that there will be some kind of change that will allow them to stay in this country. Some of them can't wait another day because they need income to help them survive, and so they are forced to do illegal things, such as forging papers and working under the table in order to stay in the country. It is a very sad situation indeed.

I think the government knows the problem, but I don't think that the average American knows how immigrants become polarized and how the system becomes complicated, and can't even help immigrants who are willing to come forward with their paperwork.

During President Ronald Regan's administration there was hope that there would be a significant change in the immigration policy when millions of immigrants were allowed to obtain a green card. I know the immigrant community is grateful to this day for his help.

In recent years, America has become a tough place to work and to make a living for a lot of immigrants. First, many do not have any way to make a living beyond manual labor. Secondly, we have to learn English, and that takes a lot of time. After we pick up a couple of English phrases like "how are you?" "Good morning," "excuse me," "sorry," and "thank you," then we start to open our eyes and find a better way to express ourselves and to adapt to the system.

Most immigrants are not well-educated people, but they do make a difference by picking up the jobs that most Americans won't do, either because they are low-paying or unsavory. For example, in the Washington D.C, Maryland, and Virginia area, immigrants come from over 100 different countries including China, Ethiopia, Eritrea, Sudan, Morocco, El Salvador, Mexico, Pakistan and India. These immigrants change the face of the capital city and have an enormous effect on the economy, working in different sectors like private industry, schools, community health, and public transportation such as taxis and limousines. Without immigrants, the low-paying jobs like farm help, bussing tables, dishwashing, and housekeeping would not be filled.

The United States is getting a more varied economically from the flow of immigrants. Most Americans are much more in favor of highly skilled immigrants because they are coming with a variety of skills.

America also helped many immigrants to become educated but most of them choose to leave America because of uncertain and tangled immigration laws.

Immigrants have a great impact on the American economy. When the economy is strong, we get great work opportunities. We see "Help Wanted" signs everywhere. That is the sign that America still needs more workers and more celebration.

The early immigrant celebration began during 1621 when natives and immigrants broke bread together in a three day celebration. During the first Thanksgiving Day, the native Indians brought roast turkeys and the colonists learned how to cook cranberries and different kinds of corn. They also learned to appreciate each other on this day for gratitude. The first President of United States, George Washington, suggested November 26 as Thanksgiving Day. Two and a half centuries later, in 1863, the event was commemorated when Abraham Lincoln called for a national day of thanksgiving, an event we now celebrate as "Thanksgiving Day."

The flow of immigrants to the United States has doubled since people realized how freedom and opportunities are wide open here for immigrants. For many immigrants, their dreams have come true. America has been supportive for hard-working immigrants and their families. In another way, immigrants help this country to move forward by working hard and paying their taxes and doing their part. We all can agree on this: the American economy has profited from the contribution of immigrants in many ways.

When I entered America in 1994, I don't recall hearing about immigration problems in the media very often. The media only discussed immigration when an immigrant broke the law. While, I also don't remember any mention of the many immigrants who were obeying the law, but now thing is changed for the most part the media seemed to be unfriendly toward immigrants.

The media is powerful in our time. People learn almost everything they know from the news. For some Americans, the media is their best friend. The American people have a wide variety of sources to learn about what is happening in America and the world, and they get it 24/7. You miss nothing.

All of the popular media sources like ABC, CBS, CNN, Fox News, MSNBC etc., have interesting debates on different issues. But in recent years, many debates center on immigrants. In other words, immigrants used to live in a friendly atmosphere, but now we are able to witness attacks on immigrants in media.

The media has focused on undocumented immigrants. The immigration issue has become extremely controversial, and the term "illegal immigrant" also has become a buzzword that immediately evokes emotion, either positive or negative. Different talk shows are always debating about undocumented immigrants, especially in election seasons.

In the 2004, 2008 and 2012 presidential races; both parties were campaigning for change in immigration laws and debating how to solve the problem. Government officials speak out openly more than they used to, and the media comments and debates with different groups. It seems that everybody is interested in how to solve the current immigration law, but still it is all out on the table.

Thomas Jefferson, speaking of immigrants and the definition of a free society, said, "Emigration to America, were the free inhabitant of the British dominions in Europe, and possessed a right which nature has given to all men, of departing from the country which chance has placed them, and going to new habitations, and there establishing new societies, seems most likely to promote public happiness, laws and regulations for this great nation."

America has a lot of immigrants because America benefits from immigrants. During John F. Kennedy's presidency the immigration issue took center stage in American politics. President John F. Kennedy was passionate about the issue of immigration reform. He believed that America is a nation of people who value both tradition and the exploration of new frontiers, people who deserve the freedom to build lives for themselves in their adopted homeland.

President Kennedy wrote a book titled *Nation of Immigrants* where he addressed immigration and the secret of America. He wrote:

This was the secret of America: a nation of people with the fresh memory of old traditions who dare to explore new frontiers, people eager to build lives for themselves in a spacious society that did not restrict their freedom of choice and action.

President Kennedy genuinely believed immigrants eased the way for other immigrant groups by doing their part. They founded and offered educational opportunities to children of later immigrants of other tongues and helped America achieve a brighter future.

In 1965, President Lyndon Johnson also said the following about immigrants: "Our beautiful America was built by strangers". From a hundred different places or more they have poured forth into an empty land, joining and blending in one mighty and irresistible tide. The land flourished because it was fed from so many sources it was nourished by so many cultures and tradition people." But now little is said about that.

We can learn a great deal from the great American leaders, such as Thomas Jefferson, Abraham Lincoln, John F. Kennedy, Lyndon Johnson, Ronald Regan and many more.

They understand immigrants, who they are, why they are here, and why Americans want them. All these questions were raised a long time ago. But the great leaders of this nation sent a clear message to all of us to remind us America is a free country, a land of opportunity. They knew when they opened their arms to welcome all immigrants that the immigrants came here for opportunities and to be part of the growing economy.

Immigration is a part of basic human dignity. It should be a right for people who are sincerely seeking work to support their families. I sincerely believe immigration is a safety net for people displaced by tragedy, and I think it should be accepted by any government. I'm mindful that any person can't just walk in and demand recognition.

However, I'm for those who are fleeing religious intolerance, sincerely seeking work and running from the brutal abuse of dictators. I believe America, as a welcoming nation can offer them the hope of a better way of life where they cherish freedom and opportunity.

I think there is a miscommunication as well as misrepresentation about immigrants in American media, especially some TV and radio programs such as FOX NEWS, CNN, and conservative radio talk shows. All of these shows talk most frequently about undocumented immigrants.

Most of the conversation in their talk shows centers on illegal immigrants. Unfortunately, when immigrants get in trouble, the debate usually centers on mass immigration, not on individual immigrants. President Regan believed that society should not blame the many for the act of an individual. I think President Reagan is right: documented or undocumented immigrants are not and should not be responsible for the act of an individual immigrant. If any undocumented immigrant, a so-call "illegal," got in trouble, the debate becomes heated and focused solely on Latinos. If the media wants to blame immigrants for the act of an individual immigrant, they should be more inclusive, including immigrants from different parts of the world, such as Ireland, Germany, France, Norway, China, Japan, South Korea, Iraq, and many more countries.

There has also been a recent backlash against immigrants in America. This turn of events is very unfortunate because America is, at heart, a very welcoming country when it comes to newcomers. In large part, the problem stems from the activities of certain Hispanic advocates and organizations. They staged massive demonstrations when Congress was debating an important immigration bill. These demonstrations were mostly by people from Mexico, El Salvador and other parts of Latin America. The crowds displayed the flags of their native countries – but there were very few American flags.

I think many Americans were insulted by this lack of respect for America. These demonstrators focused too much on their own specific groups.

I think a more integrated approach would have had a very different impact on the citizens of America. Instead of making the demonstrations almost exclusively Hispanic, it should have been far more inclusive. Immigrants from all around the world, who are enjoying the freedom and opportunity in this great nation, should have played a major role. At the same time, the American people would be reminded of their own heritage: that we all came here from other countries, or at least our ancestors did. It would reinforce our national belief that we all share one common goal: to be the best Americans that we can be.

If we remind America in this manner; believe me, the American people would start showing sympathy and support for all immigrants. If they were really told the truth, they would understand and appreciate that, first and foremost, America is a nation of immigrants. People would respond in a positive way regarding how to solve the problem.

President Bush proposed part of the solution, but he couldn't push it because his poll numbers were low and the public's interest in helping immigrants at that point in history was also low, because bashing immigrants became more popular than the president anticipated.

When the president was seeking a comprehensive immigration bill, some members of the media stood against the president's proposal, which they painted as amnesty. They stressed the idea of amnesty to influence American people to change their minds about this bill. Some of them are fair and balanced, but some of them are out of touch. They never explain to the American people the positive side of immigrants.

More or less, some members of the media have been throwing gasoline on the fire in the middle of the debate about the comprehensive immigration bill that President Bush had proposed. Some in the media work hard to find common ground on the issue. But some media and interest groups never recognized for a second the suffering and frustration of these desperate people.

Immigrants are suffering like never before, especially since September 11, 2001. Immigrants have become polarized, shamed, and caught in the middle of what happened to over 3,000 people in one single day. It was a sad day for the entire world, especially here in the United States.

As we know immigrants have a proud tradition of serving in the United State army. Following this tradition, after September 2011 thousands of men and women joined the army who were not born in the United States. Nevertheless, they are dedicated to sacrificing their lives for this great nation. I think the media has an obligation to acknowledge to American people the stories of brave immigrant soldiers.

Frankly, the media has a responsibility to explain to the American people why immigrants are facing an uphill challenge with the current immigration law. Still, there is a question that remains: Why do we have a high number of undocumented immigrants? This is a legitimate question that needs to be addressed and debated fairly enough in order to find common ground if we have any hope of solving this problem.

American people need to be reminded about our immigrant roots and how America became the land of immigrants. We have a history, and it is a history of a people who are all immigrants. Do you know why America has been blessed with its mix of culture? It's because we know how to work together and live together: all Americans who are one nation under God. I think it's one of the reasons why America has reached its high status as a powerful nation in the world.

President George W. Bush emphasized in one of his speeches, "I know many of you have a parent or grandparents who came here from another country with dreams of a better life. You know what freedom meant to them, you know that America is a more hopeful country because of their hard work and sacrifice. We honor the heritage of all no matter where they come from, because we trust in our country's genius for making us all Americans one nation under God."

We need to work together to educate the public about the value and necessity of immigrants. Then one of these days they would acknowl-edge —hey, my mom is from Italy; hey, my dad is Irish; hey, my grand-mother is from Pakistan; hey, my grandfather is from Germany; hey, my great grandmother is from Mexico; or hey, my great grandmother is from Africa. Then they will understand what their immigrant roots mean to them.

The American people need to be told the truth about American im-migrants who contributed great things and made headlines such as Albert Einstein, a German immigrant who became an American citizen in 1940 and then won the Nobel Prize for Physics.

Google's co-founder Sergey Mikhaylovich Brin immigrated to the United States from Soviet Union at the age of six. He earned his un-dergraduate degree at the University of Maryland, following his family footstep studying Mathematics, as well as computer science. After his graduation he moved to Stanford University to pursue PhD in com-puter science where he met Larry Page, whom he later became friends and business partner.

Sergey Brin story become one of the success of immigrants in America stories that made it to Forbes list of 2007, richest Americans with more than $18 billion.

Felix Frankfurter, a member of the Supreme Court, was born in Vienna, Austria in 1882 and moved with his family to the United States in 1894. He went to Harvard University and CUNY the City University of New York . In 1906 he was appointed to assistant U.S. Attorney in New

York, and later he became a teacher at Harvard Law School, where he earned a reputation as a leading Constitutional scholar.

Frankfurter advised president Roosevelt on those selected to lead agencies established during the New Deal. Frankfurter also participated in the creation of a lot of legislation before he was nominated for associate justice of the Supreme Court by President Roosevelt in 1935. After he contributed tremendous achievements and worked hard for his country, immigrant Frankfurter died in1965.

Czechoslovakian immigrant Madeline Albright is one of the great American immigrant success stories, playing a key role in the United State government and becoming the first woman to serve as Secretary of State. Today she is a professor of International Relations at Georgetown University.

Henry Kissinger, a recipient of the Nobel peace prize, is a German immigrant and American political diplomat. He served his nation as National Security Adviser and later as Secretary of State during the administrations of Presidents Richard Nixon and Gerald Ford. After his term, his opinion was still sought by many presidents and world leaders.

Robert Goizueta was born into a prominent family in Havana, Cuba. After beginning as a student in Havana, he eventually became the CEO and president of the Coca-Cola Company. Under the direction of Goizueta, Coca-Cola became a top US corporation. He is credited with invigorating the company with a global vision that helped turn Coca-Cola into a leading brand. His story is an inspiration to many Cuban Americans and too many immigrants around the world.

Popular singer and actor Frank Sinatra was the son of Italian immigrants. Beginning his musical career in the swing era, he became an unprecedentedly successful solo artist. Frank Sinatra also forged a successful career as a film actor, wining Academy Awards and many Grammy Awards, including a lifetime Achievement Grammy.

Andy Garcia was born in Havana Cuba. He is a son of immigrants from Cuba. He became known in the late 1980's and 1990's, having appeared in several successful Hollywood films, including The Godfather. Now Andy Garcia is a famous Hollywood star.

Arnold Schwarzenegger, a movie star and the thirty eighth governor of California, is an Austrian immigrant who became a citizen in 1983. Boston Red Sox baseball player Manny Ramirez is a Dominican Republic immigrant who became a citizen in 2004.

Hakeem Olajuwon, born in Lagos, Nigeria in 1963, is considered by some to be the most famous continental African to have played in any sport in the entire American continent. Olajuwon was super star as his young age in Nigeria National Basketball team. He came to America to attend University of Houston, where he led his team to three consecutive NCAA Final Four. In 1984, he signed in to Houston Rockets NBA team. Olajuwon earned a nickname "The Dream". In 1994-1995 he led Houston Rockets to the NBA championship, and voted for MVP. Olajuwon before he retired from NBA in 2002, he became an American citizen in 1993.

Alek Wek, who emigrated from Sudan, became a famous model in the United State, developed her own line design handbags, and became the first African American to be on the cover of *Elle Magazine*.

Cristeta Comeford is the White House's executive chef for President Bush and President Obama. She is the White House's first female executive chef and the first minority to hold the position. She was born in the Philippines.

There are many and many more immigrants who have helped and continue to help move this great nation forward. If we look at it closely, every aspect of the American economy has profited from the contributions of immigrants. As a matter of fact, most high tech companies that we know such as Google, Yahoo, Intel, and eBay were all founded by immigrants.

My book and my views are focused on the positive view of America and how America is a great country for all of us. But some immigrants make it difficult for those who are working hard, making a living, and trying to reach their dreams. I believe that there are a small number of immigrants who do not respect the law and are committing crimes like murder, rape, and other horrible things. There is no excuse for them, and they need to face the justice they deserve for their horrible acts. Criminal immigrants who have broken their promise to America should be punished and deported. That is fair and justice. American people must see these law-breaking immigrants as criminals. They are the bad side of the immigrant dream. We must be able to judge the difference between good and bad people. Criminal immigrants don't represent us and our values. The government needs to separate the good from the bad. We have seen a lot of immigrants who show their love and respect for America and try to protect her from enemies by joining the army, going to war, and sacrificing their lives.

We cannot deny how much America benefits from hardworking immigrants. The contribution of immigrants can be seen in every aspect of our national life. We have seen it in religion, in politics, in business, in education, and in entertainment. There is no part of our nation that has not been touched by hard working immigrants.

The failure of federal government to act on a comprehensive immigration bill forces states to adopt un-constitutional and inhumane state laws. Arizona is one of the states that passed a law making it a crime to be present in the state without legal status and give power to the police to question immigrants if they are documented or undocumented immigrants based on a suspicion that they might be illegal immigrants. I don't know how the police can identify what an illegal immigrant looks like and how accurate they will be in executing these measures.

It remains to be seen how this situation will play out.

Everybody in God's eyes is legal. Many Latinos feel they are the main target of this law. Some believe that Latinos are the new Jews of the 21st century, and some fear what happened to African Americans in the past will be repeated for them. I think this law is misguided for a lot of reasons. Targeting Latinos will not solve the problem. There are millions of undocumented immigrants coming from all over the globe, even from the neighboring country of Canada.

Following in Arizona's footsteps, Georgia, Utah, Indiana, South Carolina and Alabama were prompted by the failure of congress to pass a comprehensive immigration bill to enact their own immigration laws. Most of the states legislatures said it was very important for them to implement a law needed to protect states from the flow of immigrants into their states. However, supporters and opponents alike agree none contained provisions as strict as those passed in Alabama. One provision in the law even required schools to check each student's immigration status from kindergarten to high school. The law asked students to provide proof that they are documented or legal immigrants. An opponent of the Alabama laws says the law is designed to intimidate children who have constitutional rights to go to school whether or not they are documented.

At first glance, Alabama seems ill-suited to be the nation's immigration battleground. It's not a border State and is home to fewer undocumented immigrants than several other Southern States who have a real problem with undocumented immigrants.

The nation's strictest immigration law has resurrected ugly images from its days as the battleground state for harsh segregation laws toward the Civil Rights movement. The actions of the state's lawmakers drag Alabama to the forefront of the nation's collective memory of its violent past with segregation.

Alabama's and other few states new immigration law is a punitive and mean-spirited law. It's wrong because it's not only hurting new comers, it's hurting the image of the United States. Immigrants and some law enforcement agencies, worry the law could encourage racial profiling, drain vital and scarce law enforcement resources and could hamper more serious crime investigation and could cripple the relations with the immigrant communities. If States adopted their own laws could only make matters worse and unfairly target immigrants and also could tarnish the image of United States. Allowing such discretionary state authority would hurt and disrupt existing cooperative efforts between United States and other nations.

The Supreme Court upholding its most controversial provision "Show me your paper" but the court blocked others on the grounds that they interfered with the federal government's role in setting immigration policy and also the court rejected criminal penalties for undocumented immigrants seeking work.

The Supreme Court mixed decision does not seems likely to unleash a new wave of legislation by other states to crack down undocumented immigrants. The ruling is likely to set a new debate for long term and real immigration reform.

President Obama said "No America should ever live under a cloud of suspicion just because of what they look like". The President also emphasized his concern regard to "show me your paper" provision that could lead to racial profiling, an issue that the court may yet consider in a future case.

The Arizona law and its imitators in other states make suspects out of people based on their accent and skin should not have a place in a nation of immigrants like the United States.

America must stand for tolerance, inclusiveness, and equality, which do not violate any civil rights. There are a great number of immigrants became citizens but they don't speak English; probably the new law may violate their right as an America by targeting their accent. These kinds of immigration laws will lead to racial profiling and spread fear in immigrant communities for both documented and undocumented immigrants who helped build this great nation which has made one nation out of many people. The success of America depends upon helping newcomers assimilate into our society and embrace our common identity as Americans.

We, as a nation have to be compassionate, and we need to come together solve the problems we are facing. Some undocumented immigrants living in the United States may have earned the right to become legal. We must determine to recognize their good behavior. Otherwise, this immigration problem, with over 11 million undocumented immigrants in the country, is going to remain for the next generation as an unsolved and growing issue.

Nobody wants to see immigrants living in fear. We have to help hardworking immigrants maintain their freedom. Instead of calling people illegal immigrants, let's face the immigration problem head on with solutions that go far beyond name-calling. We can take legal action before we wait too long to act, and we must help immigrants to maintain their freedom. We have to act now. The more we ignore this problem, the more the problem grows.

America means a lot to millions of immigrants. Immigrants love America and want to live in America because of the freedom and opportunities we enjoy here—freedom and opportunities we cannot find in our homelands. American people have been kind, generous, and supportive to millions of immigrants; there is no doubt that there is no better place for immigrants than America.

America deserves a President who works to solve the problem, not to put the problem on hold and pass it to the next generation. The American people deserve to hear the facts about the broken immigration system and the role of immigrants in the American economy. People also need to be informed about the myriad contributions that immigrants make to America and what kind of benefits this great nation gets from immigrants.

God bless his heart, President George W. Bush worked hard to find a way to reward the immigrants not with amnesty but with a comprehensive immigration bill. The president went on TV and directly spoke to the American people and Congress about his immigration reform bill.

President Bush praised the American people for how welcoming and grateful we are, and he reminded Americans that America is a land of immigrants. America has always been the great hope on the horizon, an open door to the future, a blessed and Promised Land for all President Bush also said we are a nation of laws, and we are also a nation of immigrants, and we must uphold that tradition, which has strengthened our country in so many ways. These are not contradictory goals. America can be a lawful society and a welcoming society at the same time.

Before he concluded his speech, the President endorsed the comprehensive immigration reform act 2007, and he asked the American people to support his comprehensive bill.

Americans may ask why we have to change the current immigration law. My answer is our state of immigration is broken; we have to change it because the current immigration law is not sufficient. It cannot be enforced properly in order to cut the number of undocumented immigrants or, for that matter, to solve the problem we are facing.

Since I've been here over sixteen years, I have my own idea on how to cut the number of undocumented immigrants. All I have is an idea. I am not a genius, Harvard student, or an experienced government bureaucrat, but I have been in this situation as an immigrant for so long. What I know, I have learned through experience. I want to share some thoughts with the American people about immigrants. While it is not my job to tell the government how to solve the problem, I believe it is my right to speak about it.

While President Obama is trying to push comprehensive immigration bill, the momentum unfortunately is not on the immigrant's side. I am sure the support for this bill declined because it becomes extremely controversial and most Americans are getting negative information about immigrants.

If Americans received positive information, I think they would agree with the proposal that the President made. It would be so much easier for the President to solve the problem, and the nation would be safer if we could have everybody documented and fingerprinted.

The immigration issue is way beyond what the media and some members of Congress interpret it to be. The state of our immigration system is broken. I think far better solution, of course, would be for congress to pass comprehensive reform bill.

Congress should not do their job to satisfy special interest groups and lobbyists. The best thing Congress can do is lay out the facts, consult with the American people, and take decisive action to solve the problem once and for all. I think the decision Congress made to kill the comprehensive immigration reform act was not good, and in years to come, they will be held accountable by the American people.

Creature of God

We all arrive on this earth as a gift from God, a gift which allows us to be His creatures with certain rights and obligations. History tells us that some human beings never get God's message in that they never see themselves obligated in any way to others. We each start out with our own separate agendas, but without a trust in God, our gift on earth is wasted. It is every person's obligation to try to ensure human rights. These are rights not given to us by any nation or government, but by God. It should be our choice as well as our obligation that no person's rule can have authority over natural rights.

The American Declaration of Independence espoused a unique idea in the eighteenth century. It said, "All men are created equal." And that they are "endowed with the inalienable rights of Life, Liberty and the Pursuit of Happiness." This was an odd concept for the eighteenth century, but it is accepted as the ideal all over the world today.

Conscience should never be compromised on the human rights level. Yet, we are separating people into various socio-economic levels, such as rich, poor, white, or black, and into the many different world religions. This is being done in order to strip people of human rights. So, it can be seen that the modern world is much more complicated than our ideals.

Mankind has suffered and bled for so long, and yet we have gained little. We cannot continue to accept political intolerance, which, we all agree, is despotic, wicked, and given to bitter and bloody persecutions. During these chaotic conflicts, the tensions in many societies have reached a boiling point; man is seeking his long-lost liberty through blood-shed and slaughter. To the Western mind, it is inconceivable that the agitation of the Muslims should even reach our peaceful shores. Americans will have different opinions on the best ways to make America safe depending on how much they fear a Muslim invasion.

When we try to understand our disagreements in different matters, we should accept that it is natural that we have differences of opinion. We were never meant to all share the same values and principles.

Selfishness and greed also have diminished the people. The power of money has become the guiding influence in our daily lives, resulting in the poor being left behind, working hard just to survive and the rich monopolizing the world's resources for their own benefit. There is nothing wrong with becoming wealthy, whether or not you work hard to earn your money. In fact, gaining wealth is the goal of all who labor in a capitalistic system.

The problem is, when you become rich and powerful, it seems to be human nature to lose all empathy for the poor and the suffering of the world. In fact greed and selfishness become their guidelines. Some use their power and money to brutalize others and to take away their rights.

This, of course, breeds revolution. Nations that abuse their power and ignore people's rights, advance their own causes and seek destinies beyond the reach of morality, and this always leads to bloodshed. When you do not have law and do not live by rules of law, you are not a civilized society.

Freedom loving people should stand and secure freedom when it's taken away by anyone. Without liberty, life itself is futile. Most people in undeveloped countries live under a dictator's rule of law. If there is no freedom, there is no law of course, desecrating human rights. There is no recourse for the citizen who is helpless. The government has all of the power, the guns, the prisons, and the torture chambers. Repressive governments use them to keep their people in line. So, the efforts of the free nations should go beyond encouragement. It should be demanded by the free nations of the world that governments protect their own citizens. If this was required and enforced, it would eliminate much conflict, trouble, and human suffering. Also, it might help any nation to create a free society without warfare and violence. Each country would have a strong government that respects the rule of law and respects human rights. People would live happily together on their own soil, creating everything to sustain life.

This might sound like a surreal Utopia and an impossible dream. If so, why do so many countries, like America and those in Europe, now enjoy such freedom? Because the people of those countries demanded it.

Freedom is a gift of God. If we let freedom reign, our future becomes hopeful. In fact, it becomes brighter than ever before. As we know, developed countries have already earned their freedom. They have learned that the key solution is to let human beings be free.

We have endeavored to cultivate the friendship of all nations and especially those with whom we share geographical and economical self-interests. These are countries with which we want to have the most important relations. If we consider countries friends, working together as a team, we will find that it behooves our interests in every way for these countries to develop in freedom and to become prosperous on their own. This alone will eliminate conflict at all levels. Nations will be able to accelerate their independence and will share their freedom, understanding of democratic principles.

Most of the third world countries have advanced to secure their sovereignty but they have failed to secure human rights, free speech, or free elections. Basically, they are still denying freedom to their own citizens. This is why people flee from their own homeland, scattering all over the world seeking a refuge, for their safety and to fulfill lost opportunities and to find freedom.

It is amazing to read what the Bible says about immigration:

"The foreigner residing among you must be treated as your native-born. Love them as yourself, for you were foreigners in Egypt. I am the LORD your God." (Leviticus 19:34, NIV) We should pursue God's message and the freedom which is our God given rights; we should engage to help immigrants who are seeking freedom as an escape from dictators and religious intolerance. America and some European countries deserve credit for helping refugees to fulfill their dreams. They are doing exactly what God told them to do.

I can't give you the exact number but countries around the world are dramatically changing their positions and marching for freedom, which is, after all, in their own best interest, as a democratic nation will strive for unity and world peace.

Democracy gives nations the blessings of its own natural resources and the resources of its people. Hard work and the benefit of all its strength, peace, and friendship will be extended to all friendly nations, and everyone involved will benefit.

A country can't achieve freedom overnight. True liberty and justice inevitably requires a long struggle and rigorous debate. Eventually, freedom will reign throughout the world because it is the birthright and the natural condition for all of mankind.

Free Country and Land
of Opportunity

America has had a reputation since its early days as a welcoming country for immigrants, a land of prosperity and opportunity. It has a unique place in the world. Indeed, if we look at American history, the first great wave of immigrants began in the early nineteenth century when hundreds of thousands of Europeans made their way to America's shores. Some came to escape punishment for their religious beliefs, others to claim their own land.

But the ebb and flow of America's immigration story began much, much earlier. The first immigrants to enter this country were Asians who made their way across the Bering land bridge some 20,000 years ago. They then immigrated south and became, over time, what we now know as the Native Americans. And much later Vikings, conquistadors, European settlers, and slaves followed in a whole series of different and fascinating waves of immigration.

In 1492, Christopher Columbus, an Italian admiral in the employ of Spain, sailed with a diverse crew—Irish, English, Jews, blacks, and others were present aboard his three ships that traveled from Palos to the Bahamas. Christopher Columbus and other European adventurers made round trip voyages in the years that followed, prospecting, settling, and cultivating friends and enemies that changed the land and the culture of America forever.

America soon became a land of immigrants originating, at first, from Northern Europe and then traveling, in the beginning of the twentieth century, from Southern and Eastern Europe.

America is a land of immigrants; citizens of this nation were immigrants from the start. America was itself composed of a diverse population whose members came from Europe, as well as from African nations, Asia, South America, the Middle East and many more from around the globe. A huge wave of immigrants arrived in the wake of downward business cycles and famines in Eastern Europe, as well as during times of persecution. About 15 million people entered the country from Ireland, Portugal, Britain and German.

Another wave of immigration hit between the 1900s and 1920s with almost 18 million people arriving from Italy, Austria, Hungary and Russia. Today, the immigrant stream comes from literally every corner of the globe.

Many believe that one of America's strengths is derived from this diverse mix of people and cultures. It can be seen that what one culture lacks, another abounds in, thus strengthening the host country. Yes, some believe that America is successful because she is blessed with diversity.

These days, the way immigrants enter America has changed. The government began to change their quotas for entry from each country. I don't know if the average American knew about it. Every year, the government launches its Diversity Visa (DV) program which makes 55,000 immigrant visas available through a lottery to people who come from countries with low immigration quotas.

The Diversity Visa is basically a lottery for immigrants. While we have difficulty with the number of immigrants seeking legal work papers here, this dilemma does not slow down the flow of immigrants. There are great numbers of immigrants who have been here for years, have worked hard for this great nation, and who have brought prosperity to their families, but they are not still recognized by the government. They are living as "illegal immigrants" because of the uncertainty of tangled immigration laws.

The Diversity Visa (DV) lottery is an open option for everybody. This program does not discriminate against any one religion, race, sex, or age, which is a good thing as long as evil people are not able to take advantage of it. Yet, the fact of the matter is that, even with this lottery, some potential immigrants don't have the financial means to immigrate to the United States or even pay for their airplane tickets. Where I came from, it is extremely expensive to pay the ticket price to get here. Most of the people can't afford this, so their only option is to sell their lottery winning to someone who can afford it.

I leave this issue to the government and the American people. As we know, this program is designed to help countries that have low immigration quotas. If we truly want to help these lottery winners, the government should pay their way here. The government should be responsible for their expenses. I congratulate those who got the chance to come to America through this program, but I have a problem with the immigration law concerning this program.

Before they launch the DV program, they need to ask for more fully sufficient paperwork. All I'm trying to do is to remind this administration or the next administration to keep us safe. I'm not demanding that they should stop this program, but I'm asking that this Diversity Visa program be made more secure, fair, and accurate.

I have met a lot of people here in the United States who have come from different countries like Asia, Eastern Europe, Mexico, Africa, and the Middle East. They all feel strongly about their American citizenship. Almost all realize the opportunity available in this great nation.

That's why we are proud to call ourselves Americans. I am sure no one wants to voluntarily leave America unless they have no choice.

Immigrants play a central role in the cycle of the economic growth for large metropolitan's area like New York, Boston, Saint Louis, Washington D.C, Chicago and many other cities. If you look at what feeds the core of American large cities or urban areas, it is the growth of diversity and the arrival of newcomers.

Before any one derides immigrants, they have to realize the contribution of immigrants in this economy. I'm not talking about all immigrants; we have to understand that we do not come from the same countries or have the same backgrounds. We have different ambitions and dreams. I am speaking out for those who:

- Are trying to make a difference in their lives

- Believe that America is a great country for all immigrants

- Believe that America is the land of opportunity

- Believe that they have to live by the rules of the law

- Are participating to secure the freedom of this great nation

-Love America as they love themselves

American people didn't turn their backs on the decent immigrants. Hard-working immigrants are the backbone of the United State; they are part of this society. They, will work hard and answer any call their country asks them to do to prosper this great nation.

After the Fateful Day

Immigrants have a tough time living in America when they are separated from family and friends. They have left their loved ones for a
simple reason and that is to make a difference and to live in a free
country. Most newcomers realize now that without freedom, there
is no security. Without security, there is no job; it is tough to make a
living in these circumstances. Most of us understand that, if we want
to live free in this country, we have to stand up against our common
enemies. The majority of Americans understand who our enemies
are, such as Al Qaeda similar terrorist groups. These terrorists make us
afraid to speak loudly about our feelings. They are almost separating
us from who we are.

On 9/11, we watched the horror on television of what happened to
the Twin Towers and the Pentagon. A great number of immigrants lost
their lives along with innocent American people. Over 3,000 innocent
human lives were lost in one day. That reminds us that our enemies
will do whatever it takes to destroy us and has declared all out war
against us. But since 9/11, everybody has come together. The United
States is more united than ever. America fought back and committed
to hunt these extreme terrorist groups until they meet the justice they
deserve.

The action that our President took back then reminds us that there is a lot more work to do to completely defeat our enemies so that they cannot come back to attack us again.

September 11, 2001 has become the toughest day for many immigrants to associate with ordinary American people. Especially people who immigrated from part of a Muslim community and who are caught in the middle so that they cannot even express how they feel polarized and shamed about what happened on that fateful day. It was a sad day for the entire world, especially here in the United States. It was a terrible time in our history.

After September 11, 2001, many immigrants who arrived from the Middle East and parts of the Arab world did not feel comfortable enough to identify themselves. Even when asked where they were from, few would answer truthfully. One of the days after September 11, 2001, I was in a convenience store getting some juice, and this Egyptian guy walked in.

I asked him where he was from, simply because I wanted to have a conversation with him, and he told me he was from France. I told him that I didn't believe he was from France, but rather that he was from North Africa or the Middle East.

He said, "You are right. I am from Egypt, but I am scared to tell anybody because they might think I am a terrorist."

He also said, "My friend, it does not look good. These people did terrible things, and they make us look like we are the enemy of this country."

He further said, "I do not like this. I hope that the blood of innocent people hunts them. God may punish them."

And what he said wasn't too far from what I heard in the news tragically, some Americans killed an Indian man one night. They had apparently never seen anyone who looked like him before, and they were bitter and angry about 9/11.

This Egyptian man said to me, "Bye, I got to go now. Be careful." That was the last time I talked to him.

I believe that some in the press need to recognize how the life of immigrants changed after 9/11.

Freedom makes it possible for us to speak our minds. We don't want to see anybody or any group shake our will for freedom. We are all here because it's a free country and a land of opportunity. We will not give up our opportunities and our freedom for anybody. We will do whatever it takes to protect our freedom.

Most immigrants are looking for opportunities to show their support and how much they love America. They can make a difference by participating in hunting down terrorists, joining the army, and reporting:

- What they hear.

- What they observe.

- Who terrorists are.

- How terrorists get financial support.

I have not seen the government take positive steps to get the answers to all these questions. The Homeland Security Department should work closely with immigrants to learn what they know, but some members of Congress and government officials do not want to give a chance to some immigrants. And that is why many are perceived as illegal immigrants.

I think immigrants should take this opportunity, to do everything they can to help this great nation to fight against terrorist groups. I believe some immigrants do have information because some of them stay in contact with their homeland, friends, and family members. They hear things before the average American might know about them. I believe there is a golden opportunity there. But, of course, they don't come forward to give the information because they are scared that they might face deportation. This is the biggest stress that every immigrant in the United States lives with.

The problem of the broken immigration system is not only a problem for immigrants it's also a problem of security for this great nation. I believe after September 2011, it is increasingly becoming clear that it's more about our national security. I think it is essential to talk about it and take some necessary actions.

Recently luck saved countless innocent people from the New- York Time Square bomber by the action of an ordinary person who for-tuitously happened to be there at the right time at the right place. Another terrorist bomber tried to blow up a commercial airliner over Detroit on Christmas Day and he happened to be stopped by the same kind of luck. There is also a concern about homegrown terror activities. It is alarming. We need to consider all options to defeat homegrown terrorists who are encouraged by Al Qaeda, Al Shabab, and other ter-rorist groups. At this time we do not know where our enemies are, how they got here, or when they are going to attack us. We can't depend on luck or assume that we can simply continue with business as usual. We have to be cautious and vigilant, we may not be as lucky as we have been in the past.

We have to learn from our mistakes. We're not vulnerable but we need to take tough security measures and need to leave our differences behind. This problem is not only about immigration it's also about our national security. We must finger print everybody in order to find out who is coming and who staying in the country. The solutions are in our hands. It is time to find a way to solve the problem. We should stand shoulder to shoulder and come together to bring this dilemma to an end.

There is no doubt; we have a broken immigration system along with broken borders, leaving many citizens fearing for our national security. We should step up and debate about it in order to find some common ground to solve this problem.

I was curious to know how bad the system was. When I was searching regarding "catch and release" immigration enforcement. I found that our Border Patrol has worked hard to protect our borders. But sometimes there are a lot of immigrants who have to cross the border. Even as they cross the border, law enforcement cannot hold them back because they said they are not a threat, furthermore we do not have the facilities to jail them all. Instead, the government provides them with transportation to go to the bus station or wherever they want to go. It's irresponsible and totally unacceptable. I hope they changed the existing conditions.

By the time the immigrants find their destination, they have to go back to the government to ask for an I.D. The government does not let them have the I.D because, once again, it considers them illegal immigrants. Under some state laws, undocumented immigrants are not allowed to have any kind of I.D. If the government provides them transportation to go wherever they want to go, why can't the government provide them with some sort of I.D.?

We have to realize these immigrants are human beings. They need to feed themselves to survive. If they do not have an I.D, card they can't work. If they do not have jobs, there is no way for them to make a living. I believe the government forces them to do illegal things such as forging papers or working under the table without paying taxes and committing crimes such as robbery and related act. I want to fi nd out who we have to blame right now—the government or the immigrants?

Even president Bush acknowledged these problems in his speech about "catch and release". He said "For many years the government did not have enough space in our detention facilities to hold them while the legal process unfolds, most immigrants were released back into our society and asked to return for a court date. When the date arrived, the vast majority did not show up". This practice, called "catch and release," is unacceptable and the President promised to end "catch and release" once and for all.

President Obama also openly spoke about our broken immigration laws and how the tangled law impacts our national security. President Obama advocated for a comprehensive immigration bill during a campaign speech. Now the new administration has signaled its interest in a new comprehensive immigration bill. Time will tell if the American people support it. President Bush and President Obama understood that this bill is not only about immigration, it's also about national security.

Ideology of Hate

In our generation multi-millionaires have emerged as the biggest enemy of United State. After the fall of Hitler, religious zealot Osama Bin Laden supports the ideology of radical Islam. Bin Laden had money was also capable of raising money from extremists to pursue his insane ideology.

I think Bin Laden dreamed to be the most revered hero of the Islamic world. To further his goal, he bought a safe haven where he could recruit followers for his insane ideology. Time after time, his ideology has seemed to resonate with his followers. He started with a group of terrorists, which eventually evolved into a worldwide terror network "Al Qaeda."

Osama Bin Laden was always two steps ahead of the rest of Mujahedeen movement. The movement has struggled for a long time to enforce the law of Sharia, an ancient law wholeheartedly accepted by fanatical Muslim religionists. Sharia requires every Muslim nation to follow the law of the Koran. Some Muslim nations follow the rule of law of Sharia, but some do not enforce it.

Mujahedeen groups want to enforce the rule of Sharia by terrorizing and killing. According to the Koran, it is harem (prohibited) for Muslims to kill Muslims. Yet, Bin Laden found one small item that all Muslims can agree with and that is to increase the hatred of America through-out the Islamic world. He encouraged all Muslims to stand up against America, and he was able to carry that message to his followers.

The Muslim world hates Israel, and we know America is best friends with Israel, thus intensifying the hatred of both. Bin Laden got a real opportunity to fire up the Islamic world to stand against America. He started his demands for the withdrawal of all Western (infidel) troops from the sacred soil of Saudi Arabia. He was not known at that time, but he had strong connections with the Mujahedeen movement.

Every year, the most devout of Islam make the pilgrimage to Mecca in Saudi Arabia for Hajj. Mecca is the holiest of holy places for the Islamic world. In Mecca, no other religion except Islam is welcome. Even the roads leading to Mecca are divided for Muslim and non-Muslim.

Extreme radicals began demanding that America leave Saudi Arabia. This was, of course, a great opportunity for Bin Laden after America rescued the Saudi royals and the Kuwaitis from Saddam's greed. With his great wealth, it was not too difficult to recruit people and gather followers. The Saudi government got tired of Bin Laden and banished him from Saudi Arabia, but he was able to buy safe haven in Sudan.

Osama Bin Laden's movement started being recognized once he es-tablished his organization in Sudan. Sudan provided him with ev-erything he needed. He invested money in terrorist training camps and was able to make connections with different groups of radical movements.

He felt Sudan was the right place for him. He recruited his followers from Saudi Arabia, Egypt, Jordan, Afghanistan, Morocco, Pakistan, and Yemen. His organization, al Qaeda, became known around the world, and his ideology began flowing to his followers, thanks to the Sudanese leaders.

Sudan is geographically one of the largest countries in Africa. It borders the Central Africa Republic, the Democratic Republic of Chad,
and Egypt. Nearby are Eritrea, Ethiopia, Kenya, Libya and Uganda.
The Sudanese population is one of the most diverse on the African
continent. Sudan became independent 1956 from British.

Sudan was considered part of the Arab world's geographically. But
there are two major cultures Arab and Black Africans (Juba) in Sudan.
For over forty years the country has been in a Civil War between
southern Christians and the central government. For a long time in
the history of Sudan the two sides have been separated by a military
dictatorship. After a long war between the Northern Sudan central
Government and the Sudanese People's Liberation Army (SPLA) the
two sides agreed to peace under the terms of a comprehensive peace
agreement (CPA) in 2005.

A referendum took place to give southern Sudan a chance to secede
from the rest of the Sudan. The referendum was held from Jan 9 to Jan
15, 2011. After the vote, south Sudan became an Independent state on
July 9, 2011. On July 14, 2011, the new nation became a United Nations
member state.

Islamic politician named Hassan Al Turabi from the start want to overthrow his elected brother-in-law, Sudan Prime Minister Sadiq Al Mahdi
for his National Islamic movement. In 1989 with help of the military
junta Turabi succeed to oust his brother in-law from power. From the
beginning, Turabi realized he needed money for his National Islamic
Front (NIF) Movement. The NIF determined that Osama Bin Laden was
going to help him financially. Turabi was neither the first, nor the last
Muslim leader determined to tap into Osama Bin Laden's pocket. Osama
seemed to agree, handing out money to Turabi. He then set out on a
scouting mission of his own to Khartoum, the capital city of Sudan.

For years, the Sudanese government had used its territory to provide
safe haven, training camps, and staging areas to numerous terrorist

organizations including Al Qaeda and the Egyptian group Islamic Jihad, as well as to Hamas and Hezbollah. In the meantime, the United
States engaged in war with Iraq to take Saddam Hussein out of Kuwait.
At this time, Turabi backed Saddam Hussein. Turabi also provided visas
to Iraqis, Afghans, Palestinians, Egyptians and terrorists from many
other countries. Sudan became a safe haven to many Islamic radical
groups.

In 1990, Turabi succeeded by collecting money from Bin Laden, and
he received oil from Iraq and Iran. At this time, Turabi was convinced
he was on the brink of exercising his power in an NIF Revolution.

Meanwhile, he got money for his NIF but he didn't realize that he was
being blamed by his neighbors for the loss of life in Algeria and Egypt.
He became suspicious of American officials. He took time to come and
explain his stance to American officials, but the more he talked, the
more it became clear that he was on a mission for Islamic Jihad. The
government of Sudan gave material support and was directly involved
in numerous terror attacks, including assisting and harboring the failed
mission to assassinate former Egyptian leader Hosni Mubarak.

In 1995, former Egyptian President Hosni Mubarak flew to Addis Ababa, Ethiopia, for a meeting of the Organization of African Unity (OAU).
He was aware that Sudanese-based Egyptian terrorists were plotting
to kill him, as they had assassinated his predecessor, Anwar Sadat. All
of the evidence indicated support from the Sudanese government.

The Saudis and perhaps the Egyptians may have been thinking along
similar lines about the need for some covert operation against Bin
Laden in Sudan. Reports reached the FBI from Sudan of two incidents
in which someone had attempted to kill Bin Laden.

It became harder and harder for Turabi to hide the Al Qaeda leader.
Meantime the former president of Egypt, Hosni Mubarak was sending
word to Khartoum to punish the terrorists in Sudan. Egypt had moved

troops and aircraft to Sudan before and had even used its air force to bomb an anti- Egyptian radio station in Khartoum.

Osama Bin Laden began to lose his confidence in Turabi, and he began to worry about his investment. He had invested over 90 million dollars in Sudan. Osama and his war-lords started to search for a better safe haven. Turabi and Bin Laden parted as friends and pledged to continue to struggle and to use Khartoum as a safe haven.

Incredibly, it is possible that Eritrea could have put a stop to or helped to avert the terrorist attack of September 11, 2001. Western countries, including the United States, did not take the motives of Bin Laden and his Al Qaeda organization seriously. Eritrean President Isaias Afwerki in 1994 had warned President Clinton's National Security Advisor, Anthony Lake, of the terrorist organization threat in Sudan. Before relocating to Afghanistan, Bin Laden tried to use Eritrea as a staging ground for terrorism along the Red Sea and beyond.

At the same time, using Sudan as a base, the new nation of Eritrea was the first victim of Bin Laden and his Al Qaeda organization. Several innocent lives were lost and properties were destroyed.

I respect the Eritrean president for confronted the terror group in battle and also for defining the threat and the growing presence of terrorist in the horn of Africa, particularly in Sudan.

Before 1994, I spent time in my birth place, Asmara, the capital city of Eritrea, and Addis Ababa, capital city of Ethiopia. I had gone back and forth to visit my family. In 1991 after a 30-year fight, Eritrea became independent from Ethiopia. Eritrean people wildly celebrated the independence and the relief from dictatorship. For at least seven days, people were kissing, hugging, and celebrating non-stop. EPLF, which is the new government in place in Eritrea, and also TPLF, the new government in place in Ethiopia, both fought hard battles to overthrow the un-elected regime of dictator, Mengistu Haile Mariam.

After the victory, both countries marched and celebrated, but there wasn't much celebration in Addis Ababa. The new government had a hard time convincing the Ethiopian people that it was the one to bring unity and prosperity to the country. Most were skeptical about it. I was able to witness a demonstration in the capital city against the new government. The Ethiopian people were not happy with the dramatic change. The people in Addis Ababa had mixed feelings, and they were worried about the separation of the two countries.

While in Eritrea, as the people were celebrating the victory, the government warned Eritrean people about Islamist terror groups. The president said, "There are still enemies trying to attack us." He warned the Eritrean people of the nature and the motive of these enemies, and he also acknowledged they were well trained, extreme, well organized. They were dangerous, and they are also threatened our country's stability. He stressed that they came from different countries, such as Palestine, Afghanistan, Yemen, Algeria, and Egypt. All these foreign fighters were supported by the Eritrean Islamic Jihad Movement. EIJM organization was helping the foreign fighters to flee from Sudan across the border into Eritrea. President Isaias Afwerki insisted that the Eritrean people are resilient and will prevail.

Eritrea and Ethiopia are located on the Horn of Africa, both countries neighboring Sudan. After what happened next door in Sudan, Osama Bin Laden began paying close attention to Eritrea and Ethiopia. I am sure that, after the trouble with Turabi, Bin Laden began focusing on his opportunities in one of these countries. Perhaps he wanted to negotiate with Eritrean Jihad (EIJM). After a while, he became interested in Eritrea. Osama knew there were numerous political organizations in Sudan, such as the Eritrean Islamic Jihad Movement (EIJM) that could deliver his message.

EIJM is the only organization that can claim to represent Muslim Eritrean grievances. EIJM was also the only organization that approximates a conventional terrorist organization. Osama saw it as a great opportunity. That is why he kept his eyes on Eritrea and confronted Eritrea, but his mission was not successful.

Osama and his partner, Turabi, got into an unsafe Situation. Turabi got nervous. Things were not working out for both men. By late 1995, Khartoum found itself in international isolation.

In 1996, Sudan expelled Bin Laden. The moderate government blamed Turabi for its past relations with terrorist organizations. Khartoum accelerated the moderation of its foreign policy and distanced itself from terrorist organizations. In order to prevent further trouble. The leadership and the people of Sudan improved their relationship with the United States. The relationships even improved to the point that the Sudanese government offered to hand over Osama Bin Laden to United States, but the Clinton Administration felt it did not have hard evidence to convict him.

Sudan continues its cooperation today, sharing intelligence and handing over suspected terror groups that might implicate high-ranking Sudanese officials. They also are arresting individuals who have had contacts with Bin Laden.

The Sudanese government dramatic changed its policy, deepened its cooperation with the United States to investigate and apprehend extremists suspected of involvement in terrorist Turabi and Bin Laden decided to relocate Al Qaeda's network to Afghanistan to reduce international pressure on the NIF and to help the Taliban finish putting another nation into the Caliphate.

Sudan, they thought, was already well on the path. Turabi was later jailed by the Sudanese military in 2002, and the NIF members largely thrown out of government positions. The next safe haven for Bin Laden and his Al Qaeda organization became Afghanistan, which is part of the Middle East. When Bin Laden started giving up on East Africa, later he found Afghanistan was a good safe haven for him with the help of the Taliban leadership. The leader of the Taliban was much like Sudan's Turabi—a religious zealot seeking to create a theocracy.

Afghanistan and Pakistan had been safe havens for terrorist groups, but now the pressure was on them in those places. Looking for new bases for their operations, al Qaeda leaders began to once again view East Africa as a breeding ground for new recruits.

Recently, according to the U.S military and counter terrorism experts, there is concern that Somalia is increasingly on a path to become the next Afghanistan. Before he got killed, Bin laden was urging Somalia to overthrow their new moderate Islamic leader and to support their jihad's leader.

Until their overthrow, the Taliban gave Bin laden and his group safe haven in Afghanistan. Many believe al Shabab is now controlled by al Qaeda-linked foreign fighters who honed their skills in Iraq and Afghanistan.

The Taliban and al Shabab moved into a power vacuum left by inconclusive civil war. Both Follow a strict law of Sharia, they share the same tactics and ideology, and both derive support by terrorizing the population. Somalia is looking more and more like a country ruled by the Taliban.

Al Shabab is copying exactly whatever the Taliban was doing in the late 1990's. Al Shabab's recently adopted tactics long used by the Afghan militants: the terror group orders households in southern Somalia to contribute a boy to the militia's ranks. Every childless family is forced to pay money to Al Shabab.

Al Qaeda's influence in the East Africa region is already apparent, with homegrown militants who have growing ties to the terror groups. The influence of Al Shabab's homegrown Somali terrorist network in America, Europe, and around the globe is dramatically growing. Al

Shabab is also encouraging the young generation to join the fight of Jihad in Somalia and Afghanistan.

Extremists are filtering out of safe havens along the Afghanistan/ Pakistan border and into east Africa, bringing sophisticated terrorist tactics, including suicide attacks. Bin Laden made it clear in his message that East Africa, including Somalia, will be their best hope in the future of Al Qaeda. New Al Qaeda leader Alyman al-Zawahiri announced that Al Shabab "joined ranks" with Al Qaeda. He said the two organizations will work together, and he elaborate that the Somalia Islamist has joined forces with his terror network.

Bin Laden created and funded the al Qaeda terror network, which was responsible for 9/11 and other terror acts in the world, including in East Africa. The Saudi Arabia native had been on the run since the American led-invasion of Afghanistan to overthrow the Taliban who harbored him, but finally he faced the justice he deserves.

President Obama said "justice has been done" after the news broke of the death of the terror leader. After he had enough intelligence, the President authorized an operation to bring Bin laden to justice with a small team of navy seals who carried out the operation. After a firefight, they killed Bin laden and took custody of his body.

President Obama called the killing of Osama Bin laden the most significant achievement in the effort to defeat Al Qaeda.

American people celebrated the killing of Bin laden and congratulated the President, the men and women of our military, our intelligence communities, and the brave American soldiers who fought until this day.

President Bush also called the operation a "momentous achievement" that marks victory in America, for people who seek peace around the world, and for all those who lost loved ones on 9/11.

To me this is a great moment in America. Once again America sent a clear message: No matter how long it takes if you a terrorist or part of a terror network, we will find you and you will face the justice you deserve.

Terror Rally in East Africa

Sudan is not the only country that was involved with this terrorist activity. Several African countries were forced to serve the terror organizations too, directly or indirectly. Most of these countries, such as Kenya, Eritrea, Ethiopia, Somalia, Tanzania, and Djibouti became the victims of these terrorist groups. Geographically, these countries neighbor each other, and most have interesting and long histories of culture and religion.

Kenya has a very diverse population that includes three African sociolinguistic groups: Bantu, Nilotic and Cushitic. Kenyans are deeply religious; most Kenyan people are Christian. About 10 percent of the population is Muslim and another 10 percent are followers of traditional African religions. Fossils found in East Africa indicate that hominids lived in the area 2.6 million years ago near a Kenyan lake. Kenya was a British colony for many years before becoming independent in 1963.

Kenya is one of the countries seen as a soft target by Al Qaeda. Terror groups have been taking advantage of Kenya's immigration and security laws, as the Al Qaeda network depends on decentralization and flexibility. Bin Laden's secretary, Wadi el Hage, established the Kenya cell in 1994. The growth of the Al Qaeda cell in Kenya made Kenyan officials nervous. Many times the government made efforts to destroy the Al Qaeda cell by apprehending several suspects in Nairobi and Mombasa. Despite these arrests, the 1998 bombing in Mombasa occurred.

There is growing evidence of an indigenous terrorist movement in Kenya. Al Qaeda struck again in Kenya. This time, it was the Paradise Hotel in Mombassa. There was also an attempt to shoot down an Israeli airplane.

The Kenyan cell of Al Qaeda and the largest radical Islamic group in Somalia, Al Ittihad Al Islamiya (AIAI), stem from the apparent mobility of some of the key leaders to move between Kenya and Somalia. AIAI is the most powerful radical group in East Africa, and it has been funded by Al Qaeda. Furthermore, the Dabaab refugee camp on the Somalia-Kenya border has been used as a training ground for Islamic extremists.

I think the attack that took place in Mombasa was retaliation. First of all, Kenya is a good friend of Israel. Furthermore, the Kenyan government banned the registration of parties based on ethnic and religious affinities. One of the parties denied registration was the Islamic party of Kenya (IPK), which received support from neighboring Sudan. Well-known radical Islamic sheik Khalid actively opposed government policies and threatened to unleash a "Holy War." The Kenyan government stripped his citizenship and he was exiled to Germany and later to Saudi Arabia.

The war against terrorism must not be seen outside the frame work of the intention of Islamic radicals in the region. Sudan's attitude toward terrorism in Kenya was unfriendly. The Sudanese government also supported ethnic and religious groups in the region.

Kenyan government formed an anti-terrorist policy to win the fight over terror groups, and the parliament of Kenya provided authorization to detain and punish suspected terrorists.

October 15, 2011 marked a dramatic turning point in the history of Kenya, particularly the Kenyan army, as the political leadership of the east Africa country announced a major military offensive against al Shabab, one of east Africa's most daring armed groups operating in war-torn Somalia.

The decision to confront al Shabab in Somalia was taken by Kenya after a spate of kidnapping and killing along the Kenyan coast and in a refugee camp receiving Somalia nationals fleeing famine and conflict.

The most immediate trigger of Kenya's offensive sparked when al Shabab kidnapped foreigner nationals near the Kenya-Somalia border, which has intensified a negative ripple effect on the tourism industry in Kenya. Tourism accounts for a crucial share of Kenyan's revenue.

It is very interesting; the Somalia people didn't object to being invaded by Kenya, as the case was with Ethiopia in 2006. There is a sizeable population of Somalis inside Kenya, who view Kenya as having been hospitable to their families.

Meanwhile, the Kenyan military forces carried out cross border air strikes against the Somali militia targets to destroy the weapons and bases of Al Shabab. The Kenyan forces acknowledged they will hit them hard wherever they are to protect our country's territorial integrity.

The hard hit Al Shabab desperately tried to survive by changing the name of their group to Islamic Emirate in order to attract more Somali people. But the Kenyan government said Al Shabab is losing ground; whatever name or brand they use, we will continue to hunt them until their capacity is degraded.

However, without the commitment of enormous resources, it may take a long time for Kenya to rebuild local institutions and address the host of cross border refugee and immigration laws that are central to an effective anti-terrorist policy.

Kenya became an important partner in the region for the United States and formed a combined joint task force with America. The United States has spent millions of dollars on anti-terrorism assistance including training Kenyan security personnel.

In the 2008 U.S election, America elected a president who has roots in Kenya. His father was from Kogelo, a small village in west Kenya. President Barack Obama offered hope and change to a lot of people in America, and, in much the same way, he became a role model for many Kenyans and other Africans.

Kenya has been struggling for a long time with poverty and terrorism, but president Obama gave Kenyans hope and something to celebrate on November 4. The people of Kenya and the government celebrated officially on his victory.

Eritrea is one of the countries that suffered repeated terror attacks by Islamic groups backed by Al Qaeda. Eritrea is located on the Horn of Africa and is bordered on the northeast by the Red Sea, on the west and northwest by Sudan, on the south by Ethiopia, and southeast by Djibouti. Asmara is the capital city of Eritrea.

Eritrean population is estimated at a little over five million, most speak Semitic or Cushitic languages. Tigrina and Arabic are the most frequently used languages for official transactions. English is a widely spoken foreign language among educated people, and Italian is also spoken among elderly people.

Eritrea is an ancient name, associated in the past with its Greek alphabet from Erythraia. In the past, Eritrea had given its name to the red sea Bahri Negash. The boundaries of modern Eritrea and the entire region were established during the European colonial period, but ancient Eritrean history, is among one of oldest African countries.

The culmination of Islamic dominance in the region peaked in 1557, when an Ottoman invasion during the time of Suleiman and under Ozidemir Basha who had conquered the province of Habesha. With the rise of Islam in the 7th century, the power of Aksum declined and the Kingdom became isolated, the Dahlak, northern and western Eritrea came under increasing control of Islamic powers based in Yemen and Beja lands in Sudan.

While the Sudanese demanded tax payment from the western lowlands of Eritreans, the Beja were often in alliance with the Arabs, who themselves established footholds along stretches of the Eritrean coastline and the Dahlak Island.

Eritrea modern history establish in 1885, after Italians colonized the country. In 1941 Eritrea was occupied by the British, and Eritrea was placed under British military control after the Italian surrender in World War II. In 1952, a United Nation resolve establishing it as an autonomous entity federating Eritrea with Ethiopia went into effect, but the resolution made no changes.

From the start of the federation, Ethiopian king Haile Slasie attempted to undercut Eritrea's independent status. In 1962 King Haile Slasie pressured the Eritrean Assembly to abolish the federation and to join the Ethiopian empire. The skimmed demand for independence Eritrean people continued. In 1991, after a 30-year battle, the dictator, Mengistu Haile Mariam, was overthrown. Eritrea emerged as independent nation.

Eritrea has a proud history that grew from its courageous demands for independence. A fight that began with a few members of Jebha and Shabia, eventually developed into guerilla style "Warsay.", the movement emerged as the Eritrean People's Liberation Front EPLF. Finally, after 30 years of heavy battle, the country accomplished its goal of freeing Eritrea to be an independent country, safeguarding its sovereignty after liberation.

Meanwhile Ethiopia recognized the right of Eritrea to hold a referendum. In a 1993 referendum supported by Ethiopia, Eritrean voted almost unanimously for independence. As a result, Eritrea officially celebrated its independence day on May 24, 1993. But the footprints left by the colonials on the border issue didn't help to stabilize the region.

The two countries hardly became good neighbors. In 1998, border disputes around the town of Badme erupted into open hostilities. This conflict ended with a peace deal in June 2000, but not before leaving both sides with tens of thousands causalities. After all of this disaster, a security zone was created to separate the two countries. A fragile truce has held, but the UN is dragging out its effort, before fulfilling its mandate.

This ongoing dispute over the demarcation of the border threatens peace. The unsolved border issue compounds problems for growth of the Eritrean economy. It was hoped that these two neighboring countries would live peacefully, helping each other after the fall of the dictatorial régime of Mengistu Haile Mariam. However, they still have ongoing problems and differences. They did not try to solve their differences through peaceful means.

Both countries need to act responsibly and maturely to solve the ongoing problems. It is hard to accept the bitterness. But the people, unfortunately, still suffer from the fight and bloodshed. Both sides need to reject the violence and embrace peace, love, and healthy relationships in order to secure a better future for the people.

In Eritrea, Muslims and Christians are living side by side and respecting each other in many parts of the country. Eritrea never gave a chance for extremists to settle in the country, but the majority of practicing Eritrean Muslims found themselves to establish political representation outside of Eritrea.

In 1983, the Jihad Tahrir Al Eritrea, al Islamiya Wataniya (Eritrean National Islam Liberation Front) was established in Sudan. The two organizations merged with three smaller groups, the Islamic Defense Committee, the Movement of Oppressed Eritrea and Al Intifada Islamiya, formed the EIJM. However, due to the collaborated efforts of the United States and Sudan, any groups affiliated with Bin laden's terror network, like EIJM, has been shut down as a result of pressure from the United States.

In the modern era, the United States played a facilitative role in the peace talks during the months leading up to the May 1991 fall of the Mengistu regime. After 9/11 the Bush administration was working hard to improve the relationship with the Eritrean government. The administration sent Secretary of Defense Donald Rumsfeld to Asmara to discuss the war on terrorism and the defense issue in the region with the Eritrean president. The two countries had a good relationship. Unfortunately the relationship between Eritrea and the United States today is seriously strained.

The relationship broke down, when the United States accused the Eritrean government of helping and harboring Somali Islamists, sparking hostile activity against Somalia's transitional government and also for attacking Djibouti. In the meantime, the U.N. imposed sanctions against Eritrea. But the Eritrean government denounced, calling the resolution "shameful" and based on "fabricated" lies mainly hatch by the Ethiopian government and the U.S. government.

American policy appears to be unfriendly with the current administration because of the support of Islamists who joined the act of terror and episodic signals of disapproval for the administration's internal problem of human rights and the Eritrean government also accuse United States for siding with Ethiopia.

Ethiopia is not considered as soft a target as other neighboring countries such as Kenya. Ethiopia has a long and interesting history. Ethiopia is located in East Africa bordering Kenya, Sudan, Somalia, Djibouti, and Eritrea. Addis Ababa is the capital city of Ethiopia.

The population in Ethiopia is also highly diverse. Most Ethiopian people speak a Semitic or Cushitic language. Amharic is the official language in Ethiopia. But in many part of the country it has been replaced by the local languages, Oromign'a and Tigrign'a. English are the most widely spoken foreign languages in Ethiopia.

Ethiopia is credited with being the original starting place of mankind. Bones over 3.2 million years old have been discovered in eastern Ethiopia. Ethiopia is the oldest independent country in Africa and also one of the oldest countries in the world. The Old Testament of the Bible tells that the Queen of Sheba visited Jerusalem. According to history, the queen had a baby from King Solomon. She named him Menelik, and her son found the Empire of Ethiopia.

Ethiopia was gradually cut off from European Christendom during a period of bitter religious confl ict that contributed to hostility towards Christianity. Traditionally, Ethiopia was considered a Christian country, but Ethiopia has more Muslims than neighboring countries like Eritrea and Djibouti. In Ethiopia, Muslims and Christians are geographically intermixed throughout the country like Eritrea. Muslims and Christians are living together and respecting each other in many parts of the country but some Islamic groups rejected the idea of the government to interfere in their religions.

Ethiopia knows all about terrorism but appears to have remained free of terrorist attacks instigated by Al Qaeda and other terrorist group. Ethiopia historically experienced several Islamic invasions, yet Islam in Ethiopia has been benign during the past century. Nonetheless, most terrorism directed against Ethiopia has been linked to Somali Islamic terror groups. Still, for the most part Ethiopian Muslims have not been receptive to Islamic radicalism.

Ethiopia, most of the time, has feared neighboring Somalia's terror group known as AIAI which is renamed as Al Shabab.

In December 2006, Ethiopian troops entered Somalia to back their Somali allies and to oust the Islamist AIAI who controlled much of southern Somalia and Mogadishu for more than six months.

Ethiopia believes that AIAI is linked to Al Qaeda, and there is evidence to support this claim. Somalia, on the other hand, claims that AIAI is not a terrorist organization. Most Somalis are convinced that Ethiopia wants only to keep Somalia weak and divided.

Some Somali people think that Ethiopia is just using this as an excuse to do the United States' task, as we know the United States shared in the bitterness with Somalia. After that, the U.S. did not get involved in activity against the terror network in Somalia.

The United States' interest in hunting members of Al Qaeda groups served well the entry of Ethiopia into the country. The United States has also played a role as an intermediary to help resolve the tension between these two neighboring countries. America and Ethiopia have common interests in the region, and the relationship between these countries appears to be strong. Ethiopia joined the coalition of the willing against terror networks. That made Ethiopia a top-notch ally of United States.

But a growing number of Ethiopians are frustrated. They believe the United States is blind to how the Ethiopian government is using democracy as a cover-up for a continuation of its power grab and intimidating Ethiopian people from exercising their right to vote and to participate in political parties.

Somalia, for many years, has been wide open for terrorist groups. The country has been without a central government since 1991, and much of the territory has been subject to serious civil strife.

Somalia's early history traces the development of the nation into an Arab sultanate, which was founded in the seventh century by a Koreishite immigrant from Yemen. Somalia's modern history began in the late nineteenth century when various European powers began to trade and establish themselves in the area. It is comprised of Italy's former trust territory of Somalia and the former British protectorate of Somaliland.

Somalia's coast on the Horn Africa has an ancient history known as ancient Arab Berberi. The Somalia's population stretches from the Gulf of Tadjoura, Djibouti, through Ugadien, Ethiopia, and down to the coastal regions of southern Kenya. Somalia, unlike many African countries, extended its population beyond its national borders.

Most of Somalia speaks the Somali language; however, Arabic, Oromo, Urdu, English, and Italian are also used extensively.

Somalia is a collapsed state where terrorists can operate beyond the rule of law. Some radical terrorist groups appear to have used the lawless country as a safe heaven, but most part of the country has not fallen in direct political control of the largest radical group who switched their name from AIAI to Islamic Court Union. Later, this terror group merged with Al Shabab. Time after time they changed their name just to keep their radical terror group alive.

For almost four years the radical Al Shabab movement has been engaged in a violent struggle with the U.N.-backed transitional government for control of Somalia, which has had no effective administration since Mohamed Siad-Barre's regime collapsed in 1991.

Al Shabab, meaning "the youth" in Arabic, is a group determined to impose the strict, Islamic law known as "Sharia" in Somalia. In 2005, the militant youth wing of the Islamic Courts Union (ICU) briefly controlled much of the Somali land south and west before being ousted in 2006 by troops from neighboring Ethiopia.

While most of the ICU's leaders fled, Al Shabab fighters under leader Ahmed Abdi Godane remained behind to wage a guerilla-style war against the Ethiopian army. The Ethiopian army remained until early 2009 when the Transitional Federal Government (TFG) took tentative control, clinging to a small part of the capital, Mogadishu. They were supported by African Union (AU) peacekeepers mainly from Uganda and Burundi.

By contrast, Al Shabab won control over much of central and southern Somalia, while their growing ties with the Al Qaeda terror network gave them valuable manpower and resources. In the meantime, Bin Laden issued a statement calling for Muslims everywhere to help the Somali mujahedeen fight effectively "until Somalia becomes an Islamic State." According to the transitional administration in Mogadishu the growing relationship with al Qaeda led to a flowing in of militant fighters from abroad.

The group has become particularly adept at using the media to announce details of attacks that it has carried out. Al Shabab is believed to number up to 7,000 armed men, with a main force of around 3,000 fighters with well-honed guerrilla fighting skills. The signs of al Qaeda's hand in the fighting are visible in the way they adapted the use of Improvised Explosive Devices, or IED's, and suicide bombings.

An execution by stone has become a public spectacle. Men are forced to grow beards. Women can't leave home without a male relative. Watching sports on TV, watching movies, and listening to music are also banded. Recently one of the al-Shabab leaders in Somalia said elections were un-Islamic and called democracy "the devils principles." I think that will tell you all you need to know about what l-Shabab stands for.

Al-Shabab wins some sympathy by positioning themselves as defenders against invading infidels, but they are losing the hearts and minds of the ordinary Somali people.

There are numerous explanations why Somalia has proven to be a more fertile environment for terrorism than it was originally believed. Recent terrorist activity makes it a real possibility that Somalia might fall into the radicals' hands. Somali lawlessness creates conditions of insecurity, extortion, kidnapping, and betrayal that contribute to the environment that is friendly to terrorist operations. Furthermore, moderate Somali residents make it exceptionally difficult for a terrorist to go unnoticed in the country.

Somalia, nonetheless, has played a role in the Islamic movement, although a specialized one. It has served primarily as a short-term transition point for the movement of people and material through Somalia into Kenya. Somalia has not yet become a safe haven for significant terrorist activity. It has not hosted terrorist training bases, and it has not proven to be a profitable recruiting ground for Al Qaeda, but Somalia remains high on the list of potential terrorist safe havens with the threat of the largest radical Islamic group in East Africa.

In recent years, the United State backed a secret program to pay Mogadishu's widely detested warlords to help track down those in Somalia with links to terrorist. On the other hand, some Somali people are really concerned, because they think the invasion of Ethiopian troops is simply Ethiopia doing the dirty work of the United States. However, the Ethiopian government dismisses this allegation and insists that they helping and protecting Somalia from terror groups by pushing them out from power and stabilizing Somalia's transitional government.

The Ethiopian government also argues that the fight in Somalia is part of keeping Ethiopia safe from the threat of the neighboring Somali terror groups.

Al-Shabab's political platform is the imposition of Islamic government in all Somali inhabited zones of the region, including eastern Ethiopia. Al-Shabab's focus has always been on Somalia's affairs with interest in global jihads. Despite the tension, however, Al-Shabab was driven from the district of Luuq by Ethiopian forces.

Al Qaeda does not have a 100 percent control in Somalia. However Sheik Hassan and some members of the group have linked to al Qaeda. Sheik Hassan Dahir Aweys claims the leader of the Islamic opposition movement promised to impose Islamic law (SHERIA). But Ahmedou ould-Abdallah U.N special envoy says Aweys doesn't even have the full support of hard-line Islamists. Sheik Awey operates in exile after pushing out a more moderate cleric who signed a peace agreement U.N backed Somalia government.

After the September 11th attack, the United States put Sheik Aweys on the terrorist watch list because he and an Islamic group he founded, AIAI, were believed to have had links to Osama Bin Laden when he was in Sudan in the early 1990s.

The United States fears Somalia could become a haven for Al Qaida and also, though Al Qaeda does seem to exist in Somalia, it does not appear to have a significant operational presence but, they working on it.

Al-Shabab has mutated from nationalist insurgents to fully fledged terrorist organization. If you look at the rhetoric and language, if you look at the web sites, and if you hear their preacher or their scholars speak, their beliefs are completely indistinguishable from al Qaeda leaders.

Al-Shabab in Somalia and the Taliban in Afghanistan have tactics that increasingly mirror each other. Those tactics worked for the Taliban until the United States' invasion.

Uganda's recent involvement in Somalia makes it unsurprising that a newly "internationalized" al Shabab would eventually target them. Al Shabab is the leading point of inquiry because of its previous threats against Uganda.

The attacks in Kampala that killed 74 people would mark the first time the group has claimed responsibility for an operation beyond the Somali border, apart from sporadic attacks across the border into northern Kenya. The African force, known as AMISOM, trying to defeat the Islamist militia in Somalia first entered Somalia in 2007 and has long consisted of Uganda and Burundian troops.

AMISOM claimed a series of successes in a recent battle against Al Shabab fighters. Due to the successes AMISOM's number of the troops grew from 12,000 to around 17,700 troops and the United Nations has stepped up equipment support. Overall, having increased military pressure is a key element to dismantling al Shabab.

In August 2011, AMISOM forces took control of the capital city, Mogadishu, and African forces claim to have captured strongholds in the southern part of Somalia. Kenya and Ethiopian troops have launched independent incursions which have intensified pressure on al Shabab. The plan is to degrade the Islamist militia and basically destroy al Shabab.

Al Qaeda operatives have used Somalia as a transition point for terrorist attacks in Kenya. There is believed to be an anti-American underground movement, but that is hard to prove because there is no functioning national government in Somalia that can respond to potential terrorist threats.

The war on terrorism is seen by local authorities primarily as an opportunity to garner Western aid. The problem in Somalia appears to be the connection between weak, corrupt states and terrorism. The United States actively engages these problems leading towards an effective effort at winning hearts and minds, increasing American outreach in the region.

Tanzania is in many ways considered a soft target for terror groups. On August 7, 1998, Al Qaida attempted to destroy the peace in the capital city of Tanzania Dar salaam, which a lot of people call "place of peace," by bombing the American embassy building. Tanzania became part of Al-Qaida's attack in east Africa. Because of Bin Laden's cowardly attack, eleven Tanzanians, eight Americans lost their lives, and many more were heavily injured. Al Qaida killed and destroyed the building but they did not destroy the Tanzanians' sprit. This act horrified Tanzanians and Americans alike and also drew condemnation from around the world in the aftermath of the bombing.

The United Republic of Tanzania was formed out of the union of two sovereign states: Tanganika and Zanzibar. The two sovereign republics formed the United Republic of Tanzania. However the government of the united republic of Tanzania is a unitary republic, consisting of the union government and the Zanaube revolutionary government. Tanzania is located in east Africa, its neighbors Kenya and Uganda are on the north Zambia, Malawi and Mozambique on the south, Rwanda, Burundi, and the Democratic Republic of Congo on west Indian ocean on east side. The population distribution in Tanzania is uneven. At this time the population in Tanzania is believed to be around 39 million.

Tanzania has an even number among Christians and Muslims; 40 percent of Muslims are Sunni and Shia, 40 percent of the Christians are Roman Catholic, Protestants, Pentecostals, Seventh Day Adventists, Jehovah Witness, and Mormons.

37 million people live on the mainland and the rest live on the Zanzibar archipelago. The capital city of Tanzania is Dar Salaam. Tanzanians has more than 126 ethnic groups and each ethnic group has its own language. The official language is Swahili. English is widely spoken in Tanzania but after gaining independence English is no longer used in the administration, parliament, or in the government. Outside the government it is now quite common to use a mix of Swahili and English.

Tanzania is home to some of the oldest human settlements unearthed by archaeologists, including fossils of early humans found in and around Olduvai Gorge in northern Tanzania, an area often referred to as "the cradle of mankind." These fossils include paranthropus bones thought to be over 2 million years old. The oldest known footprints of the immediate ancestors of Humans, the Laetoli footprints, are estimated to be about 3.6 million years old. Reaching back about 10,000 years, Tanzania is believed to have been populated by hunter-gatherer communities, probably Khoisan speaking people. Between three and five thousand years ago, they were joined by Cushites who came from the north and the Khoisan peoples were slowly absorbed into them. The Cushites introduced basic agriculture.

About 2000 years ago, Bantu-speaking people began to arrive from western Africa in a series of migrations. These groups brought and developed ironworking skills and new ideas of social and political organization.

They absorbed many of the Cushites who had preceded them, as well as most of the remaining Khoisan-speaking inhabitants. Later, pastoralists arrived whocontinued to immigrate into the area through to the 18th century.

Travelers and merchants from the Persian Gulf and Western India have visited the East African coast since early in the first millennium, especially the towns that arose all along the coasts of Kenya and Tanzania late in the millennium. But, contrary to conventional interpretations, scholars no longer believe that Arabs or Persians were significant in founding the towns. Remains of those towns' material culture demonstrate that they arose from indigenous roots, not from foreign settlement. And the language that was spoken in them, Swahili (now Tanzania's national language), is a member of the Bantu language family that spread from the northern Kenyan coast well before a significant Arab presence was felt in the region. By the beginning of the second millennium C.E., the Swahili towns conducted a thriving trade that linked Africans in the interior with trade partners throughout the Indian Ocean.

The United States has historically enjoyed a good relationship with Tanzania; especially after terrorists bombed the U.S embassy in Dar es Salaam.

The United State maintains strong allies with the Tanzanian people and built a new embassy in Dar es Salaam. The two nations pledged for a new, even stronger relationship. The United State continues to assist the Tanzanian government with a 30 million dollar assistance package covering areas such as anti-terrorism and law enforcement.

Djibouti is one of the smallest populated nations in East Africa. Djibouti looks on the war on terrorism as a blessing because it has gained attention throughout the world including the United States. During the 1991 Gulf War, Djibouti, to some extent, was viewed as a fair weather friend of America. Djibouti is an independent coastal country with port facilities and an interesting geographical strategy.

Growing French interest in the Horn of Africa took place against a backdrop of British activity in Egypt and the opening of the Suez Canal in 1869. The Red Sea was the highest potential target for French colonial rule at that time. France expanded its protectorate to include the shores of the Gulf of Tadjoura and the Somaliland. The boundaries of the protectorate, marked out in 1897 by France and Emperor Menelik II of Ethiopia, were affirmed further by agreement with Ethiopian Emperor (Ras Teferi) Haile Selassie in 1945 and 1954. Djibouti was named French Somaliland.

Djibouti has a good natural harbor and ready access to the Ethiopian highlands. During the Italian invasions of Ethiopia in 1930 and World War II, constant border skirmishes occurred between French and Italian forces. Finally, after skirmishes and fights along the border in 1957, the colony was recognized and the Djibouti people were granted considerable self-government.

In 1975, the French government began to accommodate increasingly insistent demands for independence, and the Djibouti people held their first national elections for independence in May 1977. The following month, on June 27, 1977, the Republic of Djibouti was established.

The possibility of international terrorist activity in Djibouti has long been perceived as high because of its function as the major port widely open to the interior of East Africa and the lack of resources to monitor its porous border.

Djibouti has an army and navy, but virtually no ability to patrol the coastline effectively. In effect, the government cannot reach its own border in order to secure it. Djibouti has a migrant flow from neighboring countries, which is an increasing drain on its resources.

In Djibouti, it's hard to prove if terrorist groups are operating in the country. Its importance derives from its transit capabilities rather than its potential as a base for international terrorist organizations.

After a hard look, the western nations, including the United States, finds Djibouti as the best country to serve their interests. At this time, Djibouti serves as a key United States ally in the East Africa region and also the only nation that has a United States base in sub-Saharan Africa. It hosts the military's combined joint task force for the horn Africa.

Unfortunately, turning a blind eye is a possible response to the terrorist threat, especially given the lack of resources of this nation and the rest of East Africa. These nations had terrible experiences in the past as they were colonized, and today they face fundamental problems like poverty, unstable governments, geographic strategies to which they are vulnerable, and easy access for an enemy that seeks to create terror and mass murder.

I hope in the future we learn a great deal about how to defeat our enemies. We have to be tough and steadfast to deal with the terrorist groups and we also have to extend our hand to the innocent victims who are demanding peace, love, freedom and opportunity before they become main targets of al Qaeda and their affiliates.

After 9/11, American efforts increased in East Africa, and also the absence of American representation in East Africa in the past greatly hinders the U.S. ability to assess terrorist threats and to understand the inner workings of complicated groups and important ethnic factions.

The killing of the al Qaeda leader Osama Bin laden is most significant achievement in the effort to stop terror networks from spreading around the World. The fight against terror goes on, but America has sent an unmistakable message once again: No matter how long it takes you will be held accountable for your actions, and you will face the justice you deserve.

America needs to know what is happening in East Africa and in the Middle East. This helps the United States and the rest of the world to gather enough intelligence. If this somehow succeeds, it is a win-win situation to see the terrorists defeated once and for all, and the people can freely march for freedom.

Mind and Heart

The biggest challenge facing the United States is that of winning hearts and minds. While this is not easy and takes time and commitment, it behooves America to do it sooner rather than later before any more damage is done.

If the United States succeeds, we could enjoy peace now and for the long term. The challenge that the United States faces in winning hearts and minds could lead to a new era. Instead of a constant terrorist watch, we could regain free movement within our society, living in peace and not worrying about who our enemies are. Bomb threats and terrorist activity would be a thing of the past. Everyone would benefit and so would our economic future.

The fewer enemies we have and the more friends we make, it is quite likely that our hopes for more democratic and moderate Islamic regimes will be fulfilled, and the chances for peace and freedom in the Middle East will increase. I am sure this administration has been focused on winning hearts and minds, but at the same time, it has directed a great deal of energy toward defeating radical Muslim ideology.

In my judgment, the United States government did too little to separate terrorists from the needs and concerns of innocent people. No single enemy can be a threat to a nation but a group of enemies can be a threat to a nation.

We have to put a plan in place that questions the following:

- Why are these people willing to blow themselves up?

- Are they committing suicidal attacks because they believe the ideology, or are they simply brainwashed robots?

- Are these people carrying bombs in order to kill people or because they did not have the opportunity for an education or hard for them to make living?

I think these people are vulnerable and pushed to the limit for a lot of reasons. Al Qaeda and other terror groups are misleading these people. I think al Qaeda and the other terror groups targeted and took full advantage of these poor people, training them to blow themselves up, deceptively urging them to "kill infidels" with their insidious propaganda. That is why Al Qaeda seems to be gaining followers in the Muslim word.

One doesn't have to be a rocket scientist to figure out this problem. I think it is hard to accept that it will be enough to just tell these people that the West, including the United States, cares about you and then explain an American plan and vision for the Middle East. That plan, of course, is to put in place peace and democracy.

However, I don't think this plan alone is going to be accepted in the Muslim world.

Yet, I think there is a clear opportunity here if we look at it closely and take full advantage of it.

The alternative America can propose is future economic development including infrastructure and creating jobs. First of all, America must deal with poverty; feed hungry people, educate uneducated people, and help them plan their political future. I think it's essential for the United States to solve the ongoing problem between Palestine and Israel. Indeed, this problem needs to come to an end in order to secure peace in the Middle East. After that, I'm certain countries in the Middle East will be interested in the principles of democracy. In the meantime, America can lead and participate, encouraging countries around the region to achieve their freedom.

I met this gentleman in a hookah place. Hookah looks a little like pot. They use different smoke flavors. They put a sort of a little coil on top, and, when it is ready, they puff the smoke through the pipe. Hookah is popular in the Middle East. Most Middle Eastern people don't drink or use alcohol for recreation. They go to a coffee place, sit together, and drink tea with hookah and talk about the world situation. That is part of Arab world culture.

Mr. Abdullah which I know his first name only; is a proud "Yemeni, American". He seems like a decent guy, someone you could talk to, and he was very open-minded. We were talking about the situation in the world, and he explained how he felt about terrorists. He said, "I live in fear like everyone else in this part of the world".

He suffered a flash back from a terrible time of his life and was outraged by what fellow Muslims were doing in the name of Allah.

He asked me if I knew the real meaning of Islam. I told him, "Not really." Using his hands, he tried to explain. He said Islam means peace. He asked why we can't respect what we learn during childhood. He told me that when he was a little boy growing up with his family, he learned discipline and respect for other people and prayed every day to stay close to Allah.

He shook his head and said that, today, Bin Laden and his friends have distorted the name of Islam and converts it to terror. He said in Arabic the word "Wallahi," which means "I swear to God," He also said he had many Christian friends, and none of them ever had mistreated him.

Yet, he explained that, some people are extreme. If you did not support Bin Laden, you were considered a sell-out or trader.

Mr. Abdullah told me that these extremist groups are worthless. They bring us only hate, terror, and murder. He said, "Wallahi le azib." I swear to the great god. These people who work for them, however, are not terrorists by nature. Bin Laden has money. He bought them out, provided them money to blow themselves up, pushed them to the limit—to believe in him and that he was doing the right thing; what Allah told him to do. He has deceived them.

He was dressed in his traditional clothing, including his little hat, and kept his legs crossed, one over the other, while he was smoking his Hookah. Then he told me, "I know some people who are tired of living under their family; they do not have a job and some kind of hope to move on with their lives. Some of them take any kind of offer in order to make money."

"I think money is Bin Laden best weapon that helps him to recruit suicide bombers," he said.

He told me that he had been in the United States for over seven years. He said that he is doing well and working hard to make enough money to support his family here and back in Yemen.

He said, "God bless America" We make a living in America, and I hate to see when some fellow Muslims do things such as burning flags in the name of Allah and demanding death to America. It hurts me to see such insane activity.

I continued to ask him questions.

He replied "These are evil people who distort the name of Islam. We used to worship peacefully. Now things have changed. We are seen in many American eyes as terrorists and they are suspicious of our behavior. In the same way we are suspicious of some Americans and the way they approach us.

He told me that when he wears his traditional dress, "Jelebia," anybody who sees him on the street has a bad reaction and indicates they are not comfortable with him. "They don't think I'm a good Muslim. They don't know that I love America as I love myself," he said "They did not know that I appreciate the opportunity that I am getting from this great nation," he continued, "but after September 11, everything changed. Now they think I am a terrorist, not a good citizen. It is sad."

He was puffing the hookah and shaking his head, you could see the frustration on his face. "Ah, ah," he said over and over again. He said, "I'm not feeling comfortable anymore to associate with anybody I choose to. I see the suspicion in their eyes when they look at me, especially at the airport and public transportations. I know who to blame: Bin Laden and his Al Qaeda terror network for attacking the World Trade center and many more on 9/11."

He added, "We have to do something about this." I asked him what he would like to see to happen.

He said, "We need to go to the street and show our support and sympathy to the American people, and we need to use this opportunity to tell the American people and the whole world that we are with the United States and also, that were ready to fight back against our enemies."

He also said, "We have to make sure the American people know our suffering and our struggle, and, also, we have to acknowledge to the American people that a fair number of immigrants go to the battlefield and are sacrificing their lives for this great nation. We have to show the American people our support, and that we're in this battle too."

He is a great guy that anyone can enjoy a conversation with; I really respect his mind and perspective about this dangerous situation. Before we parted, he said, "I am going to continue doing what I do—to teach my kids the good faith, not the bad faith that divides people, and I will always teach my kids to respect and understand other people and other cultures. I will do anything to change their minds and tell them that the Americans are a wonderful, humble, caring, and respectful people."

He looked at me straight in my eyes and said, "Welahy, American people are good people." That is the last time I spoke to him. I was sorry I neglected to get his phone number. He was a great guy. I hope to see him around one day.

We all understand that there are too many terror groups, but we have to be careful here not to generalize when we say all terrorists are Muslims. But all Muslims are not terrorists. I think we have to be careful not to inflame emotions and increase the tension.

I think the terrorists themselves have been terrorized by their radical, hateful leaders such as Bin Laden. He offers them nothing except hate.

Bin Laden is a master manipulator and brainwasher he indoctrinated his followers using hate as a catalyst. He was truly evil, making poor people give their lives for the sake of his insane ideology. If those in extreme terror groups have a disagreement with their leaders, I doubt they have the right to question them. These extreme terror groups are committed to doing everything they can to attack us. As we know, terrorists have declared all-out war against America. I think when the leaders gave them the order; they believed they had an obligation to carry out the mission for the name of Allah in order to get into heaven.

One out of a hundred suicide bombers might challenge them; some may ask what will be the payment for their families. I think they might respond to them by saying, "You don't have to worry about your family Allah will protect them." As we know, money is a big motivator. The money goes to brain-wash a sacrificed person's family. This horrible act which helps al Qaeda to remain active and the extremist leaders trained by Bin Laden are the new reincarnation of Hitler.

Terrorist groups are not eradicated overnight. Extreme terrorist groups could take longer to eliminate than the brain-washed terrorist. I think these brain-washed terrorists do not know what to do and where to go, except to carry out the order from al Qaeda and other terrorist leaders. I think the problem is the United States did not reach out or offer what to do and where to go to those brain-washed people.

The United States government has to find a way to reach out to those brainwashed people who have been struggling for decades to free themselves from their horrible circumstances. I think everyone will agree with me on this one: terrorists should be perceived as criminals, not as holy warriors. We know their cause and what they trying to accomplish, but when we call them holy-warriors, we encourage them to do further violence.

I am optimistic that the United State can defeat al Qaeda if it relies less on force and more on policing and intelligence to root out the terror groups by apprehending or killing key leaders. Use of military force should be reserved for quelling large, well-armed and well-organized insurgencies. I am not saying the military should not play a big role, but local forces are particularly effective because their permanent presence in the city or small town helps them gather information from local residents. As we know, the United States has the necessary instruments to execute such a plan, including winning minds and hearts to defeat terror networks.

I think it is wrong to promise yourself that you have the right, obligation, or duty to kill innocent people. Those who do so by the name of Allah will be held accountable and punished for their actions.

We can learn from history that Hitler attempted to eliminate people, but he failed. It was a long struggle, but the world united and stood against him.

Hitler was left without any choice but to eliminate himself. Certainly America succeeds eliminating Bin Laden now we need to destabilize and eliminate the terrorist networks; I'm absolutely convinced that one of these days it will happen. Sometimes history repeats for itself, but the bottom line is we have to live in reality, not in theory or insane ideology.

Defeating Evil

After a long and bumpy road, our world has become a better place due to the lessons of World War I and World War II. We have indeed learned much from history.

In the past, I have done a lot of research about the legacy left by many great leaders. Thomas Jefferson is one of the great American leaders. He is known for the Declaration of Independence. He was outspoken in his passion for freedom. Jefferson was the primary architect of America's system of freedom. He indicated in one of his great speeches that "the will of the people is the only legitimate foundation of any government." Jefferson also reminds us that the only thing that can stand by itself between the people and the government is the TRUTH. Jefferson and many other leaders fought for our freedom and our rights. Their courageous and wise leadership has contributed much to world peace and stability, helping to assure freedom for all of us.

Heroic veterans of World War II relate to us the hardships of frontline living. They are proud of their contributions toward peace and freedom. It was a wonderful effort and a great sacrifice to bring free nations together to fight against evil and evil ideologies.

Evil leaders' agendas usually involved the destruction of human rights and, in many cases, the decimation of certain "problematic" groups in favor of their own power and beliefs. One such leader was Adolph Hitler. Even though Hitler made big headlines, there were also other fascist killers, dictators who didn't make as many headlines, but more or less, they were responsible for the deaths of millions. Benito Mussolini was one of them. This socialist journalist turned from a teacher into a mass murdering dictator.

Mussolini organized teams of uniformed thugs he named "Black Shirts" who fought other political parties in the street. After a long and destructive political campaign, the Italian government fell and Mussolini gained dictatorial power from King Victor Emmanuel. After grabbing power, the Italian dictator replaced the king's guard with his own men. He also packed the parliament with his own people and set up a secret police. When the socialist leader Giacomo Matteotti spoke out, he was found murdered. Mussolini responded by making Italy a one-party state, with himself as leader, called Il Duce. He began eliminating other political opponents one by one.

Dreaming of a new Roman Empire, in 1935 Mussolini invaded Abyssinia using aircraft and poison gas. After that, he joined the "pact of steel" with Hitler and gave military support in Spain during its Civil War of the late thirties. In 1939, Mussolini invaded Albania and, in 1940, he joined the Second World War on Germany's side by attacking France. However, Military disasters in Greece and Libya forced Hitler to help Mussolini by sending troops to the Balkans and North Africa.

After his fall in 1943, Mussolini was dismissed and arrested by the King. After serving some time in various jails and places of exile, he was rescued by elite German paratroopers from a mountaintop hotel/jail. With Hitler's backing, he set up a new fascist state in northern Italy, still under German occupation, called the Salo Republic. Bent on revenge against those whom he felt had betrayed him, he executed many, including his own son-in-law, Count Ciani.

After causing the deaths of many countrymen, in April of 1945, Mussolini tried to escape into Switzerland with his mistress, Clara Petacci. They were soon captured by Italian partisans, near Lake Como and were executed. Their bodies were strung up upside down in the Piazza Loreto in Milano.

For the sake of freedom, we need to expose the horrible story of evil and dictators for what they have done to millions and millions of people throughout the world. While we enjoy our freedom, there still are murderers and dictators who are neglecting people's freedom and their human rights. We should come together with one voice to condemn these terrible acts. Some of the dictators are deposed and others still maintain to control the lives of millions and millions of people.

Idi Amin Dada was one well-known, murderous African dictator. He was a member of the small Kakuwa tribe in Uganda.

During his youth, he joined the British Army, and he got the opportunity to fight during the Second World War. His war service helped him to be characterized as a hero. He was well known in Uganda as a heavyweight boxing champion and world class rugby player. Uganda became an independent state in 1962. At that time, Idi Amin became chief of the army and air force.

In 1971, Idi Amin staged a military coup, ousting President Milton Obote, and he promoted himself to field marshal and President of Uganda for life. Behind the fancy uniform, he was a murderous thug. He murdered the husbands or boyfriends of any woman he fancied, keeping dried body parts in the fridge. He killed his own lovers and wives if he suspected adultery.

His troops were allowed to rape and kill women. An estimated 100,000 to 300,000 Ugandans were tortured and murdered during his reign. He was a close friend and ally with Libyan leader Muammar Qaddafi, and he supported the Palestine Liberation Organization (PLO). To show his support for the PLO in July of 1976, he allowed the terrorists who hijacked a French airliner carrying Jewish passengers to land in Entebbe Uganda.

To free the hostages, there were negotiation going on all over the world, but Israel ignored the negotiations and, in a classic and daring raid, rescued its citizens from Entebbe.

Qaddafi was a friend and close supporter of Ugandan dictator Idi Amin. In gratitude, Idi Amin even married Qaddafi's daughter while he was in Libya, but she then divorced him.

Qaddafi and Idi Amin shared the same tactics: murdering people to build fear among society so they could stay in power as long it takes.

Qaddafi showed his support for his friend by sending his troops to fight against Tanzania on behalf of Idi Amin. During this fight, 600 Libyan soldiers lost their lives attempting to defend the collapsing power of Idi Amin's regime.

In 1978, Tanzanian troops backed by Ugandan units rescued Uganda from the bloody butcher. In 1979, Idi Amin fled to Libya. Later, he settled in Saudi Arabia where he lived in exile until his death in 2003.

The lunatic dictator colonel Muammar Qaddafi who had been in power for over 42 years declared war against his own people most recently. He is the new face of dictators in our time.

Qaddafi was seventeen years old when he led a demonstration at school against the monarchy in favor of the anti-colonial revolution in Algeria. He was expelled from school for his action, but Qaddafi turned everything in his favor. After attending school for two years in 1963, he attended a military academy.

In 1964, King Idris al- Sanusi's government became fragile, and Qaddafi saw real opportunity based on his realization that he needed a revolution in order to control the military. In 1969, Colonel Qaddafi and his friend staged a coup, successfully taking control of the military and the country without killing a single person. In the same year Qaddafi became commander in-chief of the Libyan Armed Force at age twenty-seven.

In 1977, Colonel Qaddafi renamed the Libyan Arab Republic to Jamahiriya based on his political philosophy published in the "Green Book." Since 1979, when Gaddafi relinquished the title of Prime Minister, he has been accorded the full honorific "Brotherly leader and Guide of the first September great revolution of the Socialist People's Libyan Arab Jamahiriya" concisely as "Brother Leader and guide of the revolution" in government statements and official press releases. Qaddafi became one of the longest serving rulers in history. He was also the longest ruler of Libya since the country became an Ottoman province in 1551.

As a new leader of Libya in 1969, Qaddafi waged a campaign against Chad. He was also involved in a violent territorial dispute with neighboring Chad over the Aouzou strip, which Libya occupied in 1973. This dispute led to the Libyan invasion of the country. The dispute was settled peacefully in June 1994 when Libya withdrew troops from Chad.

Colonel Qaddafi's regime was associated with oppression of his opponents. He also participated in numerous acts of state sponsored terrorism. In early 1986 a plot organized by Libyan secret services blew up the La Belle night club in Berlin, Germany and killed 3 people, 2 of them were Americans and injured 229 people. Among the injured people, 79 of them were Americans. Qaddafi's response was often strange and erratic.

In 1986, President Ronald Regan was authorized to bomb Qaddafi. The United States Warplanes bombed a naval academy and dropped laser-guided bombs on his residence, killing one of his family members and damaging his compound.

In 1998, Qaddafi coordinated a plot against United States. He got his revenge against the U.S. when a bomb destroyed Pan Am flight 103 over Lockerbie, Scotland, killing 270 people. After a little while he realized that he was in a big trouble when the U.N. imposed sanctions against his regime. These sanctions against his regime damaged the Libyan economy badly. Qaddafi, in exchange for the lifting of U.N. sanctions, turned the two Lockerbie suspects to authorities. Dramatically, he changed his stance. All sanctions were lifted and eventually he got what he wanted.

When things got tough for him he turned around to look for alternative. He changed his stance, and he pledged to make peace with the United States in order to escape from what happen to Saddam Hussein and his sons. Qaddafi scrambled to reach out to western nations for a peaceful deal, resulting in the lifting of U.N. sanctions.

It is unfortunate and regrettable that without the wave of revolution that started in Tunisia and Egypt, Qaddafi would be in power till this day with no opponent to challenge him. However, the people of Libya rose up against him. The Libyan dictator violently turned on his own people as his regime lost control over part of the country.

Major political protesters in Libya, inspired by the events taking place in Tunisia, Egypt, and other parts of the Arab world, quickly began a general uprising that broke out in Libya against Qaddafi's regime in February 26 2011. Qaddafi lost control over most of the country and lost the confidence of Libyan people. But Qaddafi vowed to fight until the end.

He unleashed his military and police. Foreign mercenaries also joined the fight from Chad and Niger by randomly shooting at hundreds peaceful demonstrators in Tripoli the capital city of Libya and in Benghazi. Warplanes bombed different parts of the country, including children and women. "If anybody stands against me," he said "they deserve to die." He declared war against his own people.

During the following weeks, these protesters continued to gain momentum and size despite stiff resistance from the Qaddafi regime. Unlike the former Tunisian and Egypt protests, Qaddafi vowed to "fight to death" in defense of his leadership of the country. He responded to the unrest with a large-scale, violent military action in the cities of Benghazi and Tripoli. These included the use of artillery and warplanes against protesters. The death toll is reported to be approaching more than 2,000 to 30,000 people given between March 2 and September 8 according to a credible source.

Qaddafi reportedly had foreign mercenaries defend his regime. Large swaths of the country had fallen into the hands of anti-Qaddafi rebels. It is a myth that the Qaddafi regime depends on mercenaries who paid out dollar for return to killing his own people. Libyan people demonstrated peacefully, they only asked for their aspiration of freedom.

During this time of chaos, former top Libyan officials, including Qaddafi's number two man, Interior Ministers, and the former justice minister Mustafa Abdel Jalil, formed the Interim government in Benghazi. Several key ambassadors and diplomats resigned their posts in protest over Qaddafi's heavy-handed response to the demonstrators.

Many more members of the security forces had defected, including those in Tripoli who were trusty members of Qaddafi's inner circle. Cabinet members began to refuse to implement his orders. Some resigned from their positions and some distanced themselves because they believed he would fall. Qaddafi's influential Defense Minister resigned because he didn't want to carry out Qaddafi's orders to shoot Libyans. The regime reportedly jailed him because he refused to follow the order. To me he is a courageous hero. In that tough time it took a lot of guts to stand against Qaddafi, but he did it to protect his fellow citizens.

The Khamis Brigade was led by his son Khamis Qaddafi who was trained in Libya and Russia. The Khamis Brigade was the best equipped unit of the military. It was an important asset for Qaddafi and killed many rebels and civilians. Qaddafi also heavily relies on the two top generals from his own tribe. To pump up his effort to kill people, Qaddafi paid mercenaries hundreds and thousands of dollars for their service. In Nigeria advertisements for mercenaries have appeared in Newspapers.

A Serbian newspaper reported that Serbian mercenaries were among the first to kill protesting civilians. Reports from Libya confirmed that there were a great number of mercenaries from Serbia and Ukraine because Libyan pilots refused to bomb their own people. Serbian pilots took the job, flying the warplanes that bombed civilian protesters. Qaddafi used Serbian fighters when he put down a civilian uprising in the 1990's.

The international community has warned that anyone giving or executing orders to kill civilians will be prosecuted. The United Nations has referred the massacres of unarmed civilians to the International Crime Court (ICC).

France, Britain and the United States had warned Qaddafi over and over that they would resort to military means if he ignores the United Nation's resolution demanding a cease-fire. But Qaddafi ignored the U.N. resolution.

The United States and a European coalition launched military action against the Libyan regime despite Qaddafi's resistance.

President Obama said, "In the absence of an immediate end to the violence against civilians, our coalition is acting with urgency."

For the first time, the Arab leaders authorized a no fly zone to enforce on another Arab nation in order to support the coalition allies and partners as they moved to enforce the resolution. The Arab nations who supported the resolution said, "The world will not sit while more and more civilians are killed."

The United Nation's resolution enforcing a no-fly zone forced the pro-Qaddafi fighters to withdraw, and the situation became out of control. In the meantime, the Qaddafi regime crumbled. Qaddafi lost his legitimacy and the confidence of his own people. The dramatic success of the Libyan freedom fighters' push to Tripoli left Qaddafi with no option but to run away from the capital city. In august, 2011 Qaddafi was ousted from power.

On October 20, 2011 Col Muammar Qaddafi was killed after an assault near his home town of Sirte. The man who ruled Libya for 42 years was shot and wounded at the last minute. Libya's deposed leader was pulled out alive from a drain under a motorway in Sirte, his birth place, where he had been hiding like a rat with his bodyguards. Moments later, Qaddafi was beaten to death.

As we know, the attitude of dictators was, "I will fight until I die." Qaddafi didn't fight in the end. Instead, he was in a hideout, calling the rebels who rose up against his 42 years of one-man rule "rats." At the end, it appeared that he was the rat. Colonel Qaddafi's death prompted wild scenes of celebratory gunfire rage across Libya. Finally, Qaddafi's death closes the chapter of decades of dictatorial rule in Libya.

Qaddafi is not alone; there are a lot of Qaddafi's in the African countries, some of them removed from power by force. There are many dictators who are still sitting in power. They are resisting giving rights to the people. They came to power by coups in order to hold the power as lifetime president.

Africa has had more than its share of murderous, power-hungry dictators. One who fallows Idi Amin and Qaddafi's footsteps was Robert Mugabe. He trained to be a Catholic missionary in Rhodesia (Zimbabwe). In 1960, he helped the Zimbabwe African National Union (ZANU) movement, but he got in trouble for his political activity and was imprisoned for ten years. While in prison, he organized himself as a ZANU leader. After ten years, he was released from prison.

The following year, ZANU held elections, and Mugabe won, becoming prime minister. Despite assurances given in the London settlement, Mugabe turned Zimbabwe from a parliamentary democracy into a one-party socialist state. In 1980, he served as Prime Minister. In 1987, he became the first President of Zimbabwe.

In 2000, part of Mugabe's socialist ruling plan was to take land from white landowners. Mugabe gave the land to war veterans, his friends, and family members. For his unwise, magnanimous gesture, he still got a lot of opposition. But Mugabe didn't waste time. He used his police and army to beat and murder his political opponents.

Mugabe stayed in power with no opponents for over twenty-eight years. He was responsible for the deaths of 100,000 people and more who were killed by his orders.

In March 29, 2008, Zimbabweans had a chance to cast their vote. Mugabe faced the most formidable challenge from the opposition leader of the MDC party. Mugabe tried to rig the vote and possibly delay the election, including arresting and accusing election officials of undercounting his votes. The dictator was using underhanded tactics to ensure that he remained in power. The delay upset the Zimbabwean people, but the dictator was doing everything he could to hold the power.

In June 27, 2008, Mugabe held a one-man presidential run off on the heels of his campaign of torture and violence in which dozens of opposition supporters had been killed, and thousands injured and driven from their homes. Residents were forced to vote by threat of violence or arson from Mugabe supporters, who searched for anyone without a red ink-stained finger. He even ordered the abductions and arrests of opposition party members.

Mugabe defined to the world that he is a dictator, and he is unchallengeable president. The opposition party was left without any choice but to drop out from the race.

On the next day, Mugabe claimed victory, but the whole world rejected his victory. The United States was concerned and dismissed Mugabe's victory. U.S. representatives said that the election was a sham and United Kingdom expressed their frustration, arguing that the election was illegitimate.

But Mugabe ignored the demands from whole world and still maintains to hold onto power.

The economic disasters and higher unemployment under his presidency forced Mugabe to seek another alternative. In mid September 2008, after protracted negotiations by South Africa president, Robert Mugabe and Morgan Tsvangirai signed a power sharing deal. Tsvangirai is Prime Minister, and Mugabe is President. On February 2009, the MDC leader Morgan Tsvangirai was sworn in as prime Minister, and Mugabe maintained to hold the Presidency.

The following story is the one I was able to witness as a little boy in Ethiopia. I had no knowledge of politics, and I had no clue as to why they murdered and killed people. I found out later, as an adult, that these dictators did it because they are evil and love the power.

I saw things a little child should not have seen. I saw a dead body on the street because of the "red terror" that Mengistu Haile Mariam created. I saw people crying every day. All I can remember as a little boy was that army forces came to our neighborhood and arrested our neighbor with some other people from next door, stood them against the wall side-by-side, and executed them. To this day, it is still hard for me to talk about it.

An army officer, Mengistu Haile Mariam was trained in the United States, rising through his country's military ranks. He demonstrated opposition to Emperor Haile Salassie, along with his fellow members of Derg, a military junta.

In 1974, he held Majesty, Haile Sallasie, under house arrest inside the palace, and the following year, many were executed by his orders. Mengistu also ordered the assassination of the moderate Aman Andom chairman of the country's ruling Provisional Military Administrative Council (PMAC), which is Derg. The same year he authorized the killing of the 60 executive officials who were Imperial Administrators. In 1977, he was promoted to lieutenant colonel, and he killed members of his own party leaders PMAC, making himself head of state.

When things were getting tough, his response was always mass murder. To increase his power, he unleashed the bloody revolt called the "KESHIBRE" Red Terror, which he adopted from the Russian dictator Joseph Stalin, and that holocaust killed over a million people.

The campaign killed anybody who rebelled against his ideology. Terrorizing people helped him to hold on to power for at least fifteen years without any opponents.

In 1984, he established the Ethiopian Workers Party (ESEPA). He drafted a new constitution and claimed for himself the positions of President, Chairman of the party, and Chief of Staff of the Ethiopian Army. In fact, he held every position of power in the country.

Despite the pressure from EPLF and TPLF collaborated war, his army was unable to resist the fight. Finally the regime collapsed and Mengustu removed from power. The EPLF captured Asmara and the TPLF pushed deeper and deeper to capture Addis Ababa. The support from Russia ended. Russia turned its back on him after supporting him throughout his regime.

He left without any other choice but to give up. He took a deal from former United States President Jimmy Carter. He fled to Zimbabwe, where his fellow dictator and madman Robert Mugabe still shelters him. Now he is living in exile with his wife and his kids in Harare, Zimbabwe.

The Nazi leader Adolf Hitler, without any doubt, is the most infamous tyrant of the twentieth century, possibly the most evil murderer of all time. He said in his speech that "Germany would rise to become the world's dominant power." His dream was NAZI to rule the world.

He ordered the imprisonment and death of well over six million Jews and over eleven million others considered to be inferior who did not belong to "Aryan race" million of all kinds of "undesirables" ranging from gypsies to Catholics to midgets to retarded people. He also provoked the Second World War, causing estimate between thirty-five to forty five million more to die and Germany to be completely destroyed and dismembered.

Adolf Hitler, born and raised in Austria, was the son of a customs officer who was brutal to his wife and children. As a boy, his mom inspired him to become an artist. Hitler failed not once, but twice to gain admission to the Academy of Fine Arts. He was lonely and isolated; he began to develop megalomaniacal fantasies and an abiding hatred of Jews. Hitler was rejected as unfit for service by the army, but at the outbreak of the First World War, he was accepted by the reserve infantry regiment and sent to the front. Toward the end of the war, in 1916, he was badly wounded and gassed. He was a good soldier, and, in 1918, he was decorated four times, winning the Iron Cross first class.

His time in the army turned him into a militaristic nationalist, and he remained with his regiment as an army political agent. In 1919, he left the army, and, in 1920, he was made Head of Propaganda of the German Worker's Party.

With the help of an army staff officer, Hitler was elected President of the Nazi Party. In 1921, after two years, Hitler failed to take over the Bavarian government. For this political rebellion, he was convicted and sentenced to five years in prison, but he was released after nine months. Hitler started recruiting the best people in the army. The number of Nazis in parliament increased from 12 to 230, the phenom-enal growth making the Nazi Party the biggest in the Reichstag.

In 1932, the German president, aging war hero Paul Von Hindenburg, finally agreed to appoint Hitler as Chancellor. When the Reichstag was burned down, possibly by the Nazis, Hitler found an excuse to outlaw the Communist party and arrest its leaders. An enabling act gave Hitler dictatorial power for four years. He used this to dismantle all other political parties, bringing all of their offices under direct control of the Nazi Party. When Hindenburg died in 1934, Hitler took over the presidency. In the same year, Hitler started building tanks and sending troops for training.

On August 23, 1939, he concluded nonaggression pacts with the So-viet Union. The next week, Hitler invaded Poland. Honoring their trea-ties, Britain and France declared war, but there was little they could do. Poland was quickly taken, and Hitler also seized Denmark and Norway. Hitler's fast moving mechanical forces overran these countries in a new method of warfare called "blitzkrieg." These small countries were no match for the new and mighty German war machine. France fell in a matter of weeks. But most of the British Army and much of the French Army were successfully evacuated by hundreds of boats and ships from the beaches of Dunkirk.

Hitler's plan to invade England was based on his air force the Luft-waffe, and destruction of the British Royal Air Force (RAF). Even so, it would be difficult with the Royal Navy dominating the seaways and approaches. The German head of the Luftwaffe promised Hitler the RAF would be destroyed in a matter of weeks, but the Battle of Britain proved him wrong when, with the help of radar and a new fighter plane, the Spitfire, England held out.

April, 1941, Hitler invaded Yugoslavia and Greece, and, in June the same year, he tore up the non-aggression pact he had signed in 1939.

He then invaded the Soviet Union in a massive operation called Operation Barbarossa.

Although his army won spectacular victories in the field, they failed to take Moscow. The Soviets began to rigorous a huge toll on the German armies, and the Germans were surrounded and defeated at Stalingrad, sending a huge army into the Gulags of the Soviet Union, most never to return.

Meanwhile, the British had decisively beaten his elite desert Army, called the Africa Corps, in North Africa. The final battle of Tobruk ended the gains of the Germans in North Africa. Later Germany was confronted by America. That was not his choice but he vowed to face the powerful nation as enemy. Hitler promptly declared war on the United States. By 1943, the war had turned against him; on the east front, the Russian army was pushing the Germans out of Russia. Sicily had been invaded, and his Axis partner Mussolini was finished. Allied forces were pushing their way up the Italian peninsula, and British and American bombers were pounding German cities, the Americans by day and the British by night.

As the Russian and the Allies closed in on Berlin, Hitler organized to defend to the last bullet and last man. Meantime Russian artillery thundered over his head, in Berlin bunker. Finally he declared war against German people, as he believed Germany deserved to be destroyed because it had failed to live up to his expectations and his great vision.

In 1945 Hitler married his long-time mistress, Eva Braun, and the next day both committed suicide, and their bodies were burned in a funeral pyre.

Hitler was forced to kill himself because Allied soldiers stood firm to defeat his evil ideology and his regime. We thank them for their sacrifice made our world a better place. I believe we have an obligation to pass on their courage and bravery to the next generation.

Well known Dictator Saddam Hussein, born in Tikrit and orphaned at age nine was raised by his uncle. Saddam was known among his close friends to be a slow learner. He was refused entrance to the Baghdad military Academy, so, instead, he joined the Baath Socialist Party. His rite of passage was murdering a Communist politician who had stood against his uncle. Saddam volunteered to assassinate President Abdul Karim, who had overthrown the Iraqi monarchy.

The attempt failed, and Saddam was wounded in the leg. He fled to Egypt, changing his name, using his father's first name, Hussein, to avoid arrest. Later, he returned to Baghdad, where he organized the Baath Militia which seized power in 1963. Later that year, the Baath were ousted, and Saddam was sent to prison, but he managed to escape.

At first, he ruled jointly with President Ahmad Hassam, who stepped aside in 1979. Saddam then consolidated his position as head of state putting hundreds of his rivals to death. Saddam and his family took hold of all the power. He instigated an effort to make himself leader of the Arab world, using his secret police eliminated any opposition.

Saddam was asked by a journalist about the fear in Baghdad that he might torture or kill opponents of the regime.

Saddam replied, "Of course, what do you expect if they oppose my government?" This widely explains about his character.

Saddam was convinced that he could win any battle. In 1980, he invaded the Iranian oil fields but the offensive bogged down and stagnated into a costly war of attrition. Because of Saddam's orders, thousands and thousands were killed. The war ended in 1988 after eight years. In the same year, Saddam used nerve gas against his own people to northern Kurds, who opposed his rule.

He kept making history by killing, murdering, and waging war against his people and his neighbors. Saddam always loved the power of people fearing him. In 1990, he invaded Kuwait. The following year, United States led coalition drove his forces out of Kuwait. He was badly defeated by the U. S.-led coalition, but he managed to survive.

His forces terrorized the populace of Kuwait while they were withdrawing. Saddam ordered over 300 oil wells set on fire. The United Nation passed a resolution to pressure Saddam to comply with the rule, and regulation of the United Nation. But Saddam ignored everything and he threw everything into disorder. The U.N Security Council members agreed to impose sanction on Iraq because of this resolution, Saddam had been under UN sanctions for twelve years to pressure his regime, removal from power but it didn't work.

In 2003, American-led forces invaded Iraq. Saddam's army fought the first week and then gave up. In the meantime, Saddam hid in an underground tunnel, but his two sons Uday and Qusay died in a gun battle with U.S forces.

On December 15, 2003, soldiers from the fourth Infantry Division got a tip about Saddam's location. Acting on intelligence received over a period of eight months from the small Iraqi town of Ad-dawar, located near Saddam's hometown, they started a raid and discovered an underground bunker. In this bunker, tired, bearded, and disheveled was a contrite Saddam. His first words were, "I am Saddam Hussein, President of Iraq, and I am willing to negotiate."

He was the "strong man" of his time, but when the real test came, unlike his sons, Saddam chose to surrender without a fight. In the old days they said, "You can run, but you can't hide." The U.S.-led forces gave Saddam a chance to explain himself as to why he killed so many people.

He had little to say in his defense. In fact, he offered no defense, but ranted and raved about the trial being illegal because he is the President and couldn't be punished for anything. After long trial, the court found Saddam guilty. According the court order he executed in 2006.

This war is unimaginable war between the most powerful nation and coalition forces against Dictator Saddam Hussein's regime. I did not support the war without the full consent of the U.N. I did, however, I support the idea of going after a madman and his regime. I think dictator like him needs to be out of power. Iraqi people had been suffering for thirty years under his rules; the only option was left to force him out from power.

Saddam was a dangerous man who we could never understand him. I believe the war should be pointed out in the U.N. as a regime change. America should play a big role persuading the whole world about leaders who torture, abuse, and murder their own people as Saddam Hussein did. He used weapons of mass destruction to kill his own people it is sad. United States should use this fact as strong evidence to convince the whole world to stand with one voice.

I think Saddam himself is the one who invited the United States to oust him through his illegal acts in this war. Before America went to war with him, United State had a good opportunity because the U.N. Inspectors were on the ground.

The Bush administration should have let them have as much time as they needed to find weapons of mass destruction and relocate them. But the Bush administration warned Saddam over and over that he was running out of time and the U.N hasn't had enough time to do their job.

The war started and ended in less than two weeks. The United States won the war, but invading Iraq was based on the evidence presented at United Nations, and the Bush administration subsequently could not find weapon of mass destruction in Iraq. That brought the entire operation motive into question.

Even though American was not sure that there were weapons of mass destruction but the message of freedom stands strong in Iraq. America is going to go through a tough challenge in the years to come, because of unanswered questions of Weapons and mass distraction. But the people of Iraq were happy that America was there for their freedom. Now, for the first time, they are getting the opportunity for a free election, and that is a good thing.

After all, the free society of Iraq is being destroyed by terrorist attack, killings and car bombings. When the terrorists got hit so hard in Afghanistan, which was their previous safe haven, in the past years they tried to use Iraq as potential safe haven but the Iraqi people resist against terrorist.

America needs to come hand and glove to eliminate evil dictators and remove them from power. We've got to make sure that we send a clear signal. After all, this is going to be a strong message to all evil and dictators out there. I believe the war in Iraq needs to come to an end with a great dignity.

The Arab spring is the next wave of change around North Africa and the Middle East. Who could have imagined that the match young Mohamed Bouazizi lit to burn himself protesting dictatorship in Tunisia would now be torching decades-old dictatorships in Egypt, Libya, Yemen, and Syria? Could one reasonably doubt that the winds of change will not carry the embers of freedom from Tunisia and Egypt to other countries in the region?

On March 2011 the Syrian people rebelled against a decade of family rule by Basher Al Assad's regime. We have watched the horrible images in the news media as Dictator Al Assad's military forces responded to the Syrian people by bombarding demonstrators, killing women and children while the international community watched.

The Al Assad regime didn't learn from former leaders of Tunisia, Egypt and Libya. Despite the Syrian people's aspiration for a free Syria, the regime's military forces intensified their attacks on Homs and other anti-Assad strongholds. As the Syrian people desperately fought for their freedom, Al Assad's regime subjected residents in several cities to indiscriminant bombardment by tanks and rocket fire. Devastating Homs and other cities and leaving many people dead or wounded.

The violence worsened every day. The Syrian military forces and security forces launched massive campaigns of arrest, arbitrarily detentions of thousands of protesters as well as activists and others suspected of anti-government activities.

As the death toll grows in Syria, so do the desperate plea for help. The United States, the European Union, the Arab League and Turkey all called for Al Assad to step down from power, but Al Assad refused to accept the call against him. The International community pressured the regime by imposing sanctions against his regime, but the violence has only worsened.

The international community has debated over arming the opposition or providing the same kind of air support that was given to Libyan freedom fighters to stop the bloodshed in Syria. The U.N. voted against the Libyan regime in order to impose a no fly zone and the use of all necessary measures to protect the Libyan people from Qaddafi's forces. But there is no international consensus at this time since Russia and China are siding with the Assad regime.

This is the most obvious hurdle for Syrian people. There is also a big debate among the international community whether or not to arm the Syrian oppositions, but many questions still surround the Syrian opposition. Who they are? Who is in charge? Can they be trusted?

The international community will not intervene until they get a clear picture from the Syrian opposition groups about who they are and what they believe. The Syrian opposition needs to unify as one, and they need to gain some credibility in the eyes of Syrian people in order to get the support they are demanding. I'm optimistic that the regime is on its last leg. The sanctions and economic crisis will crumble the regime's ability to lead the country.

My guess is it will be very hard for the opposition groups to remove Al Assad's regime from power. Unless the Syrian opposition leaders unify and capitalize the opportunity, if not the momentum of Syrian uprising is not likely to go very smooth.

Terror and exploitation is a typical aspect of life for far too many in Africa and Middle East. Many people in America simply can't imagine the struggles that many people in Africa and Middle East face on a regular basis.

Since I grew up next to Sudan, I personally watched Omar Al Bashir oppress his own people after seizing power with a military coup in 1989. He overthrew an elected government and killed approximately 1 million people in a civil war. Darfur was plunged into turmoil in 2003, when ethnic African rebels took up arms against the Arab-dominated Sudanese government, whom they accused of discrimination.

The Sudanese dictator which is accused by International Criminal Court (ICC) of retaliating by unleashing Arab militias on civilians, the UN estimates over 500, 000 people have died and 2.7 million have been displaced in the conflict.

The Security Council authorized the court to investigate atrocities in Darfur in 2005, and it has issued an arrest warrant for the Sudanese President for allegedly orchestrating genocide, crimes against humanity and war crimes in Darfur. Under Bashir there are no independent media outlets, political parties, or parliament for that matter. Some live in a state of internal exile, while many others are abused under the brutal application of Sheria law.

While Bashir seized power illegally, other dictators took control after being democratically elected, such as Charles Taylor who was elected in 1997 in Liberia. According to Amnesty International, Taylor's army uses rape, mutilation, and torture to control the population. Many people in Liberia have essentially been reduced to slave labor while Taylor plunders all of the nation's natural resources for his own profit. As if stealing freedom from his own people isn't enough, Taylor also uses blood diamonds to fund the civil war in neighboring Sierra Leone.

For the crime he perpetrate Charles Taylor sentenced for 50 years in prison by International Criminal Court for supplying and encouraging rebels in neighboring Sierra Leone in a campaign of terror, involving murder, rape, sexual slavery and the conscription children younger than 15.He was also found guilty of using Sierra Leone diamond deposits to help fuel its civil war. As bad as life can be in a nation like Liberia, nations like Somalia have known little more than chaos and civil war for decades, sending many refugees all over the world, including the United States.

Starting in 1969, Mohamed Siad Barre seized control of Somalia and used inter-tribal warfare to divide and rule Somalia until he was overthrown in 1991. From 1988 to 1990, it is estimated by Africa Watch that approximately 50,000 to 60,000 people were killed. In addition, civilians were displaced and their livestock destroyed. The chaos that Barre helped start has continued to fester in Somalia for people who have endured this kind of brutality.

Most African dictators amended their constitutions so that no opposition leader or party could run for the presidency or other national office and have a chance to win in a fair and free election. Because African dictators live in an echo chamber, they are self-delusional. They convince themselves that they have popular support. Mubarak believes he has the full support of Egyptian people, and by reshuffling his cabinet and appointing his army buddies to top posts, he could continue his 30-year-old dictatorial rule.

Most of African dictators their attitude exposed them to be an evil. Their desire for power contributes arrogant, they believe that they can save the day by making a few superficial concessions and grandstanding promises of democratization, reorganization and reconciliation. Without the support of the West, no dictatorship in Africa could survive but some of them enjoy the support they receive from west.

Regrettably, there are far too many opposition leaders in Africa who are driven by the singular desire to grab power than are interested in bringing about real change. Truth be told, many African opposition leaders have little faith in the courage and resourcefulness of the people; and the people prove them wrong every time.

Once opposition leaders seat themselves in the saddles of power, they become the mirror images of the dictators they fought to remove. In the eyes of the people, many of these leaders have proven to be wolves in sheep's clothing; they want to grab power to make sure "it is their turn to eat, their turn at the trough." That is the reason why people in many parts of Africa have little faith in the opposition leaders or their parties. Further evidence in support of the assertion that many opposition leaders are driven by a hunger for power is their inability to present to the people concrete and comprehensive proposals to address the structural problems of poverty, unemployment, inflation, corruption, oppression and human rights violation in their countries. In short, many opposition leaders have no plans to clean up the mess the dictatorships always leave behind, and have failed to become beacons of hope to guide their people out of despair. That is what we seem to be witnessing today in Tunisia, Egypt, and Libya and elsewhere the history of the human struggle for freedom offers many lessons.

One of the great lessons of the past two decades is that political changes that ensure lasting peace and guarantee freedom and human rights do not come as a result of military or palace coups but through simple acts of civil disobedience, passive resistance and the spontaneous actions of ordinary people and youth. Of cores civil uprising and mass resistance peaceful popular uprisings is prohibited by many African dictatorships, matter fact any group or individual dare to do so might face series consequence like torture or jail time. But there is a great role to be played by individuals, small groups, civic society and other informal institutions dedicated to the defense and protection of human rights and the rule of law.

An African Charter against dictatorship is long overdue. When the mud walls of African dictatorships tumbling down, the palaces of illusion behind those walls will vanish without a trace. If Africans are to have hope of a better future and fulfill their destiny to become one with all free peoples in the world, they will need to build a fortress of freedom impregnable to the slings and arrows of civilians' dictators and the savage musketry of military juntas. African dictators should heed these words: Those who make peaceful change impossible make a violent revolution inevitable.

Africans must look to civil society institutions and grassroots organizations to spearhead real change and take charge of their destiny. The first step towards that end is for ordinary Africans committed to nonviolent peaceful change to take a stand against dictatorship openly and defiantly. It has been done before successfully a number of times, how individuals without political partisanship, affiliation or ideology -- but committed to human rights and freedom -- were able to change history by simply standing up for their beliefs and defying dictatorships.

Those who do not learn from history are doomed to repeat it but there is much to be learned from the history of African dictatorships. Africa's dictators have methodically and systematically wiped out their strongest opposition by demonizing, jailing, intimidating, torturing and outlawing them. They have neutralized rivals even with their own ranks. The dictators have created their own political institutions and doctored their constitutions to allow for change to come only through the auspices of their own parties and allies.

The history of the human struggle for freedom offers many lessons. One of the lessons I believe that political changes that ensure lasting peace and guarantee freedom and human rights can be achieve through simple acts of civil disobedience, passive resistance and the spontaneous actions of ordinary people and youth in the streets fed up with corruption, poverty, unemployment and human rights abuses.

The freedom fighters of today often become the hope of tomorrow. For those living under dictators, escape is usually the only solution. However, for those who enjoy freedom in America, we should do our part. We have an obligation to speak out and press African dictators by any means necessary to ensure freedom for African people and beyond.

For a Bright Future Together

We used to worry about the Cold War and nuclear annihilation. That dark scourge, for the most part, has been eliminated from the world scene in our generation, thanks to the leaders, President Ronald Reagan and Michael Gorbachev, who together stood hand-in-hand with the same message. The leaders of these two powerful countries understood their differences, and they decided to march for freedom to bring peace and stability because the alternative was destruction of much of the world.

While it is true that this compromise does not at first seem to be the work of divine intervention, it certainly might be. Who knows what God put in these leaders' ears or their souls in the dark fearful night? From their great leadership, their message is now spreading all over the world and has started knocking on every country's leader's door. For those who don't want to hear freedom's call, the message should be: We, the peace-loving, free people of the world demand, yes, demand that you give your people freedom.

America, more than two centuries ago, was blessed to have several great architects of the constitution, men like Thomas Jefferson, Benjamin Franklin, and all the other signers of the Constitution. At that time, the idea of people governing themselves was foreign and, frankly, scary to many, especially the monarchies of Europe.

For years, in the eighteenth century, the French resisted democracy because, in their eyes, it would be government by the rabble. That's not a very uplifting commentary on their feelings for their population, but, nevertheless, that's how they felt. And to some degree they may be right. The masses were uneducated and not given to reason.

When the French Revolution did free the masses, it also unleashed a bloody reign of terror not seen in the world since. Many, many innocent people, who were branded enemies of the state, literally lost their heads to the guillotine because their presence frightened those in power. It takes a lot of courage to carry out such a revolution because, due to human nature, one never knows exactly what dark and bloody road the revolution will follow.

Now we can see that a lot of nations understand what freedom means. They have established good relationships with the Western nations and have shown an interest in Western politics and economy. They try to use the lessons they are learning from the experience of great leaders, and we can see their countries advancing politically and economically to the level that human beings deserve. Most of their leaders are making good progress toward freedom and a free society so that freedom can flourish in their own countries.

Developed countries have a responsibility to support and help other nations who are demanding freedom. As President Franklin Roosevelt once said, "A nation, like a person, has a mind—a mind that must be kept informed and alert, that must know itself, that understands the hopes and the needs of its neighbors, all the other nations that live within the narrowing circle of the world."

A great number of countries today are willing to lead their people from darkness toward freedom but lack the means to sustain themselves while implementing a free capitalistic economy. The free nations of the world could and should help them financially, practically, and politically. The most important thing free nations can do is to encourage and support nations for their freedom and independence, while they make the transition to democracy.

In our generation, there are a lot of political partitions: communism, socialism, and democracy. There have been many hard political clashes between these competing ideologies, and the world is still debating the merits or limitations of each. The only one that seems to have truly touched people's hearts and minds is democracy.

For many nations, these terms socialism, communism, republic and democratic, are merely terms used to fool the world. For example, China is one of the repressive nations, yet calls itself the People's Democratic Republic. Everyone knows that there is nothing that is democratic about China. Nor is it a republic. It is actually a typical authoritarian and totalitarian state. Oddly enough, however, China is now catching up with the rest of the world economically and militarily; it is slowly becoming a nuclear-armed superpower. Why? Because, without saying so, the Chinese are slowly shucking the restraints of communism, which stifles trade and commerce and even human motivation, and hitching their wagon to the capitalistic system. And yet, they didn't admit any of this. If you ask a Chinese government official what kind of state China is, he will say "communist." If you ask him why the word "democratic" is in the name of the People's Republic of China, his answer will be that it is "democratic" because the people have voted for communism.

Look at North Korea. Its official name is the People's Republic of Korea. Never has there been a more repressive nation than North Korea, and look at their name. The People's Republic—as if the people have anything to do with running the country. The North Korean people are mere cogs in the wheels of the state. So saying that these countries are "democratic" is akin to saying that they have voted for slavery. Any thinking person can see through the false reasoning of those like Saddam Hussein, Muammar Qaddafi, or Robert Mugabe. If you check out the names of their countries, you will often see the word "democratic" in the title. These leaders will tell you that their people have "chosen" this form of government.

When the former Soviet Union shucked its satellite states and became modern Russia, its constitution read very much like the United States' Constitution. That is, it guaranteed all of its citizens certain rights except the Soviet Union was totalitarian. Any citizen who dared to protest using negative phrase against the state suffered repression. Sure, they said they had rights, but we must always make a sharp distinction between what any government says and what it actually does.

Democracy cherishes the principle of social equality and respects the sources of political power. It also carries a political message. In my understanding, democracy is basically a government elected by the people for the people; the people can secure certain rights.

During the American Civil War, Abraham Lincoln, in a dedication at the battlefield at Gettysburg, said in his speech, in effect, that if the union did not prevail, then government of the people, by the people, for the people would perish from the earth. And if the Union had lost, it well might have. But the Union did not lose, and America went on to become a freedom-loving nation. It offered then and, in some ways still offers, a unique opportunity among many nations.

Democracy provides free elections and the principles of freedom to all of its citizens. Elections are often regarded as synonymous with freedom. Democracy has allowed countries to have self-rule and human rights. Freedom of speech, free elections, and the rule of law are only a few of the rights guaranteed by a true democracy. Democracies also allow anybody, theoretically at least, to become a leader. However, leaders have to be chosen by their peers, the nation's population. They have to go through tough campaigns and at the end the winning candidate is the people's choice. In democratic states, the country is also allowed to have more than one political party.

Candidates are free to campaign for their group or party. People get a chance to choose a candidate. This is done without coercion, subversion, or any other pressure. In fact, such actions would be highly illegal and quickly struck down.

Democracy helps countries to elevate themselves economically and politically with respect for their own obligations and their citizens. Democracies do not tolerate discrimination or violence. The democratic process helps them to come together for their own mutual good and to guarantee freedom.

America, throughout its history, has had a commitment to democracy through good times and bad times, through peace, and through war. The attitude of a democracy is: No matter what, we will pay the ultimate price for freedom. There is a slogan being bandied about during this current War in Iraq— "Freedom is not free." Whatever your views are on this particular war, think about that powerful slogan. How true it is? Honestly, freedom is not free.

Many thousands of Americans and others have died face-down in the mud to preserve that freedom. So please, don't ever think it is free. It might have been provided for you if you have never served your country in the military, but whether you have or not, others have had to protect and preserve your freedom. We should always be thankful for their sacrifice.

America aspires to be a nation dedicated to spreading democracy around the globe. American people in the past have fought hard to preserve democracy.

So what honest person can suggest that American ideals are just that, ideals only?

Of course sometimes a democratic transition can be messy when it is hijacked by new autocrats who use violence, deception, and rigged elections to stay in power. But this is not simply a matter of idealism; it is a strategic necessity. Without genuine progress toward open and accountable political systems, the gap between people and their governments will grow, and instability will only deepen if people are forced to accept unelected regimes that hold power for an indefinite amount of time. A country can be strong if the leaders acted to meet the aspirations of the people.

Those who stand against freedom do so because it is in their best interest to restrain people from being free. If people are not free, dictators can have their way as long as possible. Free speech and public demonstrations do nothing for dictators except undermine their power, and, of course, they don't like that. These self-interested dictators are power-lovers and do not like people being free and exercising their rights.

The world has discovered that all dictators have a limited shelf life. They go as long as they can, and then it's over. They are deposed or killed. It is impossible to maintain power and keep a free-thinking people down in the depths of repression forever. Tyrants inevitably lose the support of the people; of course they lose because the strongest power is the power of the people.

In our generation, rules apply and people obey the law because the Constitution permits democracy to serve human needs and human rights.

The principles of democracy are the primary source of political power. Leaders are held accountable in a political or social unit that has a government with representatives elected by the people for the people. Democracy also allows us to maintain our rights of life, liberty, and the pursuit of happiness, as guaranteed by the Constitution. Leaders have to work for the people. Our vote is our power. No matter what elected officials do to serve us on their terms, at the end, the power comes back into our hands for the purpose of checks and balances.

It is almost as if we are the boss: we hire and fire elected officials, including the President. That is why we are determined to hold onto our freedom.

A lot of nations are struggling with their poor economies and educational systems. We have to find a way to reach out to the undeveloped countries that have been struggling for decades to feed and educate their citizens. People always want the best for themselves. As long as developed countries provide them hope and unconditional support, they will always follow the road to prosperity, but the United State cannot do it alone or start it from scratch. Undeveloped countries have a responsibility to engage in fierce debates in order to find common ground and to make a strong commitment to their bright future.

I believe Third world countries need America and the European countries help to get out of their horrible circumstances. If a nation wants to declare freedom and democracy, freedom- loving countries can make a big difference by helping these countries to achieve their goals. I am sure we would be satisfied by the outcome and success of this strong commitment. We have to encourage countries to participate in such a course of action and to be a model for the rest of nations to follow the same path.

In order to understand what's at stake for many immigrants who come to America and the importance of standing up for freedom throughout the world, we need to talk about the challenges that many people face around the world. In my own native continent of Africa, freedom can be hard to find with so many dictators brutalizing their own people and fighting to hold on to their power. We need a peaceful, diplomatic solution before more nations descend into civil wars that cause only more bloodshed and suffering.

From my own experience I believe it's the right time for nonviolent resistance and international pressure against the dictators in Africa who make life miserable for their own people. Some of these dictators are willing to partner with terrorist organizations as well; and therefore both the people of these nations and the immigrants who have moved to America want to see the United Nations step up its diplomatic pressure on dictators.

Immigrants to America such as myself know what it's like to live without freedom, and therefore we are extremely committed to both world peace and the prosperity of America.

The demand for freedom forced the regimes of Tunisia, Egypt, and Libya to step down from their positions. Ordinary people overthrew their leaders after more than thirty and forty years in power. The Egyptian people's revolution has been seen as an inspiration to the world for carrying out a non-violent revolution. Meanwhile the demand for free democracy ripples from the revolutions in Egypt, Tunisia, and Libya and continue to spread in Arab countries, perhaps around the globe.

People have become open-minded for democracy and freedom. If a lot of nations march for freedom, people all over the world will come together and respect each other, no matter what religion or culture we belong to. We believe in freedom—we all should have the chance to experience it. On the other hand, our enemies are trying to divide us, to cause people to hate each other, and to kill one another based on ideology.

In order to have a better world for years to come, we must take the lead to bring the U.N. and other nations to one table in order to defend human rights before we are hijacked by dictators or terrorists. We must push terrorists, terrorist supporters, and dictator into a corner in order to prevent them from killing and torturing people who love freedom and peace. To me, this is the challenge we have to win because it is vital to our interests. We must work hard to bring all nations to one table We need to make the U.N. active and effective. We have to change the way some countries view westerners. Let's give the opportunity to the U.N. to engage hardliners. I say, "The more friends we have, the fewer enemies we face, and the more enemies we have, the more problems we face." Even though the road to freedom is long and hard, at the end, freedom is going to rise all over the world. America and members of the United Nations will have to work hard during this generation, as well as to the next generation to bring people together. If people around the world are given the opportunity of freedom, they will come together for a better life.

For a lot of reasons, there is a lot of hate in the Middle East. Sometimes it is necessary to step aside from the conflict, but sometimes we can't step aside, if there is something that is threatening our future. We have to engage and evolve to bring peace and stability. I think that working with and within world organizations will be far more helpful than going it alone. The worst thing a country could do is to set itself apart from the rest of the world and world opinion.

We have to be careful not to do any damage by raising a higher clamor than the rest of the world's respected nations. As we know, the U.N. is not a strong organization, and it seems to me that it has failed in its message of peace and unity time after time. We need to hope, though, that this organization, in the future, could be the nations' umbrella for peace and stability. And despite having concerns and differences with the U.N., we have to take the lead and make this organization stronger than ever.

If the U.N. is to succeed in the future, we might see the U.N. increasingly reaching out to solve problems and face challenges throughout the world. Our future will be more hopeful if this happens, and fewer countries will be involved in difficult situations. Indeed, that is what will determine the success or failure of our generation. I'm optimistic, and it's possible that in the long term we could see peace, prosperity, and freedom around the world.

www.ingramcontent.com/pod-product-compliance
Lightning Source LLC
Chambersburg PA
CBHW051435280526
45785CB00003B/1293